The Enchiridion

The Enchiridion

St. Augustine

The Enchiridion

© Lighthouse Publishing 2018

Written by St. Augustine (354 – 430)

Translated by J.F Shaw (1838 – 1905)

Updated to modern U.S English by A.M Overett (1960)

All rights reserved. Without limiting the rights under copyright reserved above, no part of this publication may be reproduced, stored in a retrieval system, or transmitted, in any form or by any means (electronic, mechanical, photocopying, recording or otherwise), without the prior written permission of the copyright owner of this book.

Published by
Lighthouse Christian Publishing
SAN 257-4330
5531 Dufferin Drive
Savage, Minnesota, 55378
United States of America

www.lighthousechristianpublishing.com

Argument.

Laurentius having asked Augustin to furnish him with a handbook of Christian doctrine, containing in brief compass answers to several questions which he had proposed, Augustin shows him that these questions can be fully answered by anyone who knows the proper objects of faith, hope, and love. He then proceeds, in the first part of the work (Chap. ix.—cxiii.), to expound the objects of faith, taking as his text the Apostles' Creed; and in the course of this exposition, besides refuting divers heresies, he throws out many observations on the conduct of life. The second part of the work (Chap. cxiv. —cxvi.) treats of the objects of hope, and consists of a very brief exposition of the several petitions in the Lord's Prayer. The third and concluding part (Chap. cxvii.-cxxii.) treats of the objects of love, showing the pre-eminence of this grace in the gospel system, that it is the end of the commandment and the fulfilling of the law, and that God himself is love.

Chapter 1. —The Author Desires the Gift of True Wisdom for Laurentius.

I Cannot express, my beloved son Laurentius, the delight with which I witness your progress in knowledge, and the earnest desire I have that you should be a wise man: not one of those of whom it is said, "Where is the wise? where is the scribe? where is the disputer of this world? hath not God made foolish the wisdom of this world?" but one of those of whom it is said, "The multitude of the wise is the welfare of the world," and such as the apostles wishes those to become, whom he tells," I would have you wise unto that which is good, and simple concerning evil." Now, just as no one can exist of himself, so no one can be wise of himself, but only by the enlightening influence of Him of whom it is written," All wisdom cometh from the Lord."

Chapter 2. —The Fear of God is Man's True Wisdom.

The true wisdom of man is piety. You find this in the book of holy Job. For we read there what wisdom itself has said to man: "Behold, the fear of the Lord [pietas], that is wisdom." If you ask further what is meant in that place by pietas, the Greek calls it more definitely θεοσέβεια, that is, the worship of God. The Greeks sometimes call piety εὐσέβεια, which signifies right worship, though this, of course, refers specially to the worship of God. But when we are defining in what man's true wisdom consists, the most convenient word to use is that which distinctly expresses the fear of God. And can you, who are anxious that I should treat of great matters in few words, wish for a briefer form of expression? Or perhaps you are anxious that this expression should itself be briefly explained, and that I should unfold in a short discourse the proper mode of worshipping God?

Chapter 3. —God is to Be Worshipped Through Faith, Hope, and Love.

Now if I should answer, that God is to be worshipped with faith, hope, and love, you will at once say that this answer is too brief, and will ask me briefly to unfold the objects of each of these three graces, viz., what we are to believe, what we are to hope for, and what we are to love. And when I have done this, you will have an answer to all the questions you asked in your letter. If you have kept a copy of your letter, you can easily turn it up and read it over again: if you have not, you will have no difficulty in recalling it when I refresh your memory.

Chapter 4. —The Questions Propounded by Laurentius.

You are anxious, you say, that I should write a sort of handbook for you, which you might always keep beside you, containing answers to the questions you put, viz.: what ought to be man's chief end in life; what he ought, in view of the various heresies, chiefly to avoid; to what extent religion is supported by reason; what there is in reason that lends no support to faith, when faith stands alone; what is the starting-point, what the goal, of religion; what is the sum of the whole body of doctrine; what is the sure and proper foundation of the catholic faith. Now, undoubtedly, you will know the answers to all these questions, if you know thoroughly the proper objects of faith, hope, and love. For these must be the chief, nay, the exclusive objects of pursuit in religion. He who speaks against these is either a total stranger to the name of Christ, or is a heretic. These are to be defended by reason, which must have its starting-point either in the bodily senses or in the intuitions of the mind. And what we have neither had experience of through our bodily senses, nor have been able to reach through the intellect, must undoubtedly be believed on the testimony of those witnesses by whom the Scriptures, justly called divine, were written; and who by divine assistance were enabled, either through bodily sense or intellectual perception, to see or to foresee the things in question.

Chapter 5. —Brief Answers to These Questions.

Moreover, when the mind has been imbued with the first elements of that faith which worketh by love, it endeavors by purity of life to attain unto sight, where the pure and perfect in heart know that unspeakable beauty, the full vision of which is supreme happiness. Here surely is an answer to your question as to what is the starting-point, and what the goal: we begin in faith, and are made perfect by sight. This also is the sum of the whole body of doctrine. But the sure and proper foundation of the catholic faith is Christ. "For other foundation," says the apostle, "can no man lay than that is laid, which is Jesus Christ." Nor are we to deny that this is the proper foundation of the catholic faith, because it may be supposed that some heretics hold this in common with us. For if we carefully consider the things that pertain to Christ, we shall find that, among those heretics who call themselves Christians, Christ is present in name only: in deed and in truth He is not among them. But to show this would occupy us too long, for we should require going over all the heresies which have existed, which do exist, or which could exist, under the Christian name, and to show that this is true in the case of each, —a discussion which would occupy so many volumes as to be all but interminable.

Chapter 6. —Controversy Out of Place in a Handbook Like the Present.

Now you ask of me a handbook, that is, one that can be carried in the hand, not one to load your shelves. To return, then, to the three graces through which, as I have said, God should be worshipped—faith, hope, and love: to state what are the true and proper objects of each of these is easy. But to defend this true doctrine against the assaults of those who hold an opposite opinion, requires much fuller and more elaborate instruction. And the true way to obtain this instruction is not to have a short treatise put into one's hands, but to have a great zeal kindled in one's heart.

Chapter 7. —The Creed and the Lord's Prayer Demand the Exercise of Faith, Hope, and Love.

For you have the Creed and the Lord's Prayer. What can be briefer to hear or to read? What easier to commit to memory? When, as the result of sin, the human race was groaning under a heavy load of misery, and was in urgent need of the divine compassion, one of the prophets, anticipating the time of God's grace, declared: "And it shall come to pass, that whosoever shall call on the name of the Lord shall be delivered." Hence the Lord's Prayer. But the apostle, when, for the purpose of commending this very grace, he had quoted this prophetic testimony, immediately added: "How then shall they call on Him in whom they have not believed?" Hence the Creed. In these two you have those three graces exemplified: faith believes, hope and love pray. But without faith the two last cannot exist, and therefore we may say that faith also prays. Whence it is written: "How shall they call on Him in whom they have not believed?"

Chapter 8. —The Distinction Between Faith and Hope, and the Mutual Dependence of Faith, Hope, and Love.

Again, can anything be hoped for which is not an object of faith? It is true that a thing which is not an object of hope may be believed. What true Christian, for example, does not believe in the punishment of the wicked? And yet such an one does not hope for it. And the man who believes that punishment to be hanging over himself, and who shrinks in horror from the prospect, is more properly said to fear than to hope. And these two states of mind the poet carefully distinguishes, when he says: "Permit the fearful to have hope." Another poet, who is usually much superior to this one, makes a wrong use of the word, when he says: "If I have been able to hope for so great a grief as this." And some grammarians take this case as an example of impropriety of speech, saying, "He said sperare [to hope] instead of timere[to fear]." Accordingly, faith may have for its object evil as well as good; for both good and evil are believed, and the faith that believes them is not evil, but good. Faith, moreover, is concerned with the past, the present, and the future, all three. We believe, for example, that Christ died, — an event in the past; we believe that He is sitting at the right hand of God, —a state of things which is present; we believe that He will come to judge the quick and the dead, —an event of the future. Again, faith applies both to one's own circumstances and those of others. Everyone, for example, believes that his own existence had a beginning, and was not eternal, and he believes the same both of other men and other things. Many of our beliefs regarding religious matters, again, have reference not merely to other men, but to angels also. But hope has for its object only what is good, only what is future, and only what affects the man who entertains the hope. For these reasons, then, faith must be distinguished from hope, not merely as a matter of verbal propriety, but because they are essentially different. The fact that we do not see either what we believe or what we hope for, is all that is common to faith and hope. In the Epistle to the Hebrews, for example, faith is defined (and eminent defenders of the catholic faith have used the definition as a standard) "the evidence of things not seen." Although, should anyone say that he believes, that is, has grounded his faith, not on words, nor on witnesses, nor on any reasoning whatever, but on the direct evidence of his own senses, he would not be guilty of such an impropriety of speech as to be justly liable to the criticism, "You saw, therefore you did not believe." And hence it does not follow that an object of faith is not an object of sight. But it is better that we should use the word "faith" as the Scriptures have taught us, applying it to those things which are not seen. Concerning hope, again, the apostle says: "Hope that is seen is not hope; for what a man seeth, why doth he yet hope for? But if we hope for that we see not, then do we with patience wait for it." When, then, we believe that good is about to come, this is nothing else but to hope for it. Now what shall I say of love? Without it, faith profits nothing; and in its absence, hope cannot exist. The Apostle James says: "The devils also believe, and tremble."—that is, they, having neither hope nor love, but believing that what we love and hope for is about to come, are in terror. And so, the Apostle Paul approves and commends the "faith that worketh by love;" and this certainly cannot exist without hope. Wherefore there is no love without hope, no hope without love, and neither love nor hope without faith.

Chapter 9. —What We are to Believe. In Regard to Nature It is Not Necessary for the Christian to Know More Than that the Goodness of the Creator is the Cause of All Things.

When, then, the question is asked what we are to believe in regard to religion, it is not necessary to probe into the nature of things, as was done by those whom the Greeks call physici; nor need we be in alarm lest the Christian should be ignorant of the force and number of the elements,—the motion, and order, and eclipses of the heavenly bodies; the form of the heavens; the species and the natures of animals, plants, stones, fountains, rivers, mountains; about chronology and distances; the signs of coming storms; and a thousand other things which those philosophers either have found out, or think they have found out. For even these men themselves, endowed though they are with so much genius, burning with zeal, abounding in leisure, tracking some things by the aid of human conjecture, searching into others with the aids of history and experience, have not found out all things; and even their boasted discoveries are oftener mere guesses than certain knowledge. It is enough for the Christian to believe that the only cause of all created things, whether heavenly or earthly, whether visible or invisible, is the goodness of the Creator the one true God; and that nothing exists but Himself that does not derive its existence from Him; and that He is the Trinity—to wit, the Father, and the Son begotten of the Father, and the Holy Spirit proceeding from the same Father, but one and the same Spirit of Father and Son.

Chapter 10. —The Supremely Good Creator Made All Things Good.

By the Trinity, thus supremely and equally and unchangeably good, all things were created; and these are not supremely and equally and unchangeably good, but yet they are good, even taken separately. Taken as a whole, however, they are very good, because their ensemble constitutes the universe in all its wonderful order and beauty.

Chapter 11. —What is Called Evil in the Universe is But the Absence of Good.

And in the universe, even that which is called evil, when it is regulated and put in its own place, only enhances our admiration of the good; for we enjoy and value the good more when we compare it with the evil. For the Almighty God, who, as even the heathen acknowledge, has supreme power over all things, being Himself supremely good, would never permit the existence of anything evil among His works, if He were not so omnipotent and good that He can bring good even out of evil. For what is that which we call evil but the absence of good? In the bodies of animals, disease and wounds mean nothing but the absence of health; for when a cure is effected, that does not mean that the evils which were present—namely, the diseases and wounds—go away from the body and dwell elsewhere: they altogether cease to exist; for the wound or disease is not a substance, but a defect in the fleshly substance,—the flesh itself being a substance, and therefore something good, of which those evils—that is, privations of the good which we call health—are accidents. Just in the same way, what are called vices in the soul are nothing but privations of natural good. And when they are cured, they are not transferred elsewhere: when they cease to exist in the healthy soul, they cannot exist anywhere else.

Chapter 12. —All Beings Were Made Good, But Not Being Made Perfectly Good, are Liable to Corruption.

All things that exist, therefore, seeing that the Creator of them all is supremely good, are themselves good. But because they are not, like their Creator, supremely and unchangeably good, their good may be diminished and increased. But for good to be diminished is an evil, although, however much it may be diminished, it is necessary, if the being is to continue, that some good should remain to constitute the being. For however small or of whatever kind the being may be, the good which makes it a being cannot be destroyed without destroying the being itself. An uncorrupted nature is justly held in esteem. But if, still further, it be incorruptible, it is undoubtedly considered of still higher value. When it is corrupted, however, its corruption is an evil, because it is deprived of some sort of good. For if it be deprived of no good, it receives no injury;

but it does receive injury, therefore it is deprived of good. Therefore, so long as a being is in process of corruption, there is in it some good of which it is being deprived; and if a part of the being should remain which cannot be corrupted, this will certainly be an incorruptible being, and accordingly the process of corruption will result in the manifestation of this great good. But if it do not cease to be corrupted, neither can it cease to possess good of which corruption may deprive it. But if it should be thoroughly and completely consumed by corruption, there will then be no good left, because there will be no being. Wherefore corruption can consume the good only by consuming the being. Every being, therefore, is a good; a great good, if it cannot be corrupted; a little good, if it can: but in any case, only the foolish or ignorant will deny that it is a good. And if it be wholly consumed by corruption, then the corruption itself must cease to exist, as there is no being left in which it can dwell.

Chapter 13. —There Can Be No Evil Where There is No Good; And an Evil Man is an Evil Good.

Accordingly, there is nothing of what we call evil, if there be nothing good. But a good which is wholly without evil is a perfect good. A good, on the other hand, which contains evil is a faulty or imperfect good; and there can be no evil where there is no good. From all this we arrive at the curious result: that since every being, so far as it is a being, is good, when we say that a faulty being is an evil being, we just seem to say that what is good is evil, and that nothing but what is good can be evil, seeing that every being is good, and that no evil can exist except in a being. Nothing, then, can be evil except something which is good. And although this, when stated, seems to be a contradiction, yet the strictness of reasoning leaves us no escape from the conclusion. We must, however, beware of incurring the prophetic condemnation: "Woe unto them that call evil good, and good evil: that put darkness for light, and light for darkness: that put bitter for sweet, and sweet for bitter."1103And yet our Lord says: "An evil man out of the evil treasure of his heart bringeth forth that which is evil."1104Now, what is evil man but an evil being? for a man is a being. Now, if a man is a good thing because he is a being, what is an evil man but an evil good? Yet, when we accurately distinguish these two things, we find that it is not because he is a man that he is an evil, or because he is wicked that he is a good; but that he is a good because he is a man, and an evil because he is wicked. Whoever, then, says, "To be a man is an evil," or, "To be wicked is a good," falls under the prophetic denunciation: "Woe unto them that call evil good, and good evil!" For he condemns the work of God, which is the man, and praises the defect of man, which is the wickedness. Therefore every being, even if it be a defective one, in so far as it is a being is good, and in so far as it is defective is evil.

Chapter 14. —Good and Evil are an Exception to the Rule that Contrary Attributes Cannot Be Predicated of the Same Subject. Evil Springs Up in What is Good, and Cannot Exist Except in What is Good.

Accordingly, in the case of these contraries which we call good and evil, the rule of the logicians, that two contraries cannot be predicated at the same time of the same thing, does not hold. No weather is at the same time dark and bright: no food or drink is at the same time sweet and bitter: no body is at the same time and in the same place black and white: none is at the same time and in the same place deformed and beautiful. And this rule is found to hold in regard to many, indeed nearly all, contraries, that they cannot exist at the same time in any one thing. But although no one can doubt that good and evil are contraries, not only can they exist at the same time, but evil cannot exist without good, or in anything that is not good. Good, however, can exist without evil. For a man or an angel can exist without being wicked; but nothing can be wicked except a man or an angel: and so far as he is a man or an angel, he is good; so far as he is wicked, he is an evil. And these two contraries are so far co-existent, that if good did not exist in what is evil, neither could evil exist; because corruption could not have either a place to dwell in, or a source to spring from, if there were nothing that could be corrupted; and nothing can be corrupted except what is good, for corruption is nothing else but the destruction of good. From what is good, then, evils arose, and except in what is good they do not exist; nor was there any other source from which any evil nature could arise. For if there were, then, in so far as this was a being, it was certainly a good: and a being which was incorruptible would be a great good; and even one which was corruptible must be to some extent a good, for only by corrupting what was good in it could corruption do it harm.

Chapter 15. —The Preceding Argument is in No Wise Inconsistent with the Saying of Our Lord: "A Good Tree Cannot Bring Forth Evil Fruit."

But when we say that evil springs out of good, let it not be thought that this contradicts our Lord's saying: "A good tree cannot bring forth evil fruit." For, as He who is the Truth says, you cannot gather grapes of thorns, because grapes do not grow on thorns. But we see that on good soil both vines and thorns may be grown. And in the same way, just as an evil tree cannot bring forth good fruit, so an evil will cannot produce good works. But from the nature of man, which is good, may spring either a good or an evil will. And certainly, there was at first no source from which an evil will could spring, except the nature of angel or of man, which was good. And our Lord Himself clearly shows this in the very same place where He speaks about the tree and its fruit. For He says: "Either make the tree good, and his fruit good; or else make the tree corrupt, and his fruit corrupt,"— clearly enough warning us that evil fruits do not grow on a good tree, nor good fruits on an evil tree; but that nevertheless the ground itself, by which He meant those whom He was then addressing, might grow either kind of trees.

Chapter 16. —It is Not Essential to Man's Happiness that He Should Know the Causes of Physical Convulsions; But It Is, that He Should Know the Causes of Good and Evil.

Now, in view of these considerations, when we are pleased with that line of Maro, "Happy the man who has attained to the knowledge of the causes of things," we should not suppose that it is necessary to happiness to know the causes of the great physical convulsions, causes which lie hid in the most secret recesses of nature's kingdom, "whence comes the earthquake whose force makes the deep seas to swell and burst their barriers, and again to return upon themselves and settle down." But we ought to know the causes of good and evil as far as man may in this life know them, in order to avoid the mistakes and troubles of which this life is so full. For our aim must always be to reach that state of happiness in which no trouble shall distress us, and no error mislead us. If we must know the causes of physical convulsions, there are none which it concerns us more to know than those which affect our own health. But seeing that, in our ignorance of these, we are fain to resort to physicians, it would seem that we might bear with considerable patience our ignorance of the secrets that lie hid in the earth and heavens.

Chapter 17. —The Nature of Error. All Error is Not Hurtful, Though It is Man's Duty as Far as Possible to Avoid It.

For although we ought with the greatest possible care to avoid error, not only in great but even in little things, and although we cannot err except through ignorance, it does not follow that, if a man is ignorant of a thing, he must forthwith fall into error. That is rather the fate of the man who thinks he knows what he does not know. For he accepts what is false as if it were true, and that is the essence of error. But it is a point of very great importance what the subject is regarding which a man makes a mistake. For on one and the same subject we rightly prefer an instructed man to an ignorant one, and a man who is not in error to one who is. In the case of different subjects, however, —that is, when one man knows one thing, and another a different thing, and when what the former knows is useful, and what the latter knows is not so useful, or is actually hurtful, —who would not, regarding the things the latter knows, prefer the ignorance of the former to the knowledge of the latter? For there are points on which ignorance is better than knowledge. And in the same way, it has sometimes been an advantage to depart from the right way, —in travelling, however, not in morals. It has happened to myself to take the wrong road where two ways met, so that I did not pass by the place where an armed band of Donatists lay in wait for me. Yet I arrived at the place whither I was bent, though by a roundabout route; and when I heard of the ambush, I congratulated myself on my mistake, and gave thanks to God for it. Now, who would not rather be the traveler who made a mistake like this, than the highwayman who made no mistake? And hence, perhaps, it is that the prince of poets puts these words into the mouth of a lover in misery: "How I am undone, how I have been carried away by an evil error!" for there is an error which is good, as it not merely does no harm, but produces some actual advantage. But when we look more closely into the nature of truth, and consider that to err is just to take the false for the true, and the true for the false, or to hold what is certain as uncertain, and what is uncertain as certain, and that error in the soul is hideous and repulsive just in proportion as it appears fair and plausible when we utter it, or assent to it, saying, "Yea, yea; Nay, nay,"—surely this life that we live is wretched indeed, if only on this account, that sometimes, in order to preserve it, it is necessary to fall into error. God forbid that such should be that other life, where truth itself is the life of the soul, where no one deceives, and no one is deceived. But here men deceive and are deceived, and they are more to be pitied when they lead others astray than when they are themselves led astray by putting trust in liars. Yet so much does a rational soul shrink from what is false, and so earnestly does it struggle against error, that even those who love to deceive are most unwilling to be deceived. For the liar does not think that he errs, but that he leads another who trusts him into error. And certainly, he does not err regarding the matter about which he lies, if he himself knows the truth; but he is deceived in this, that he thinks his lie does him no harm, whereas every sin is more hurtful to the sinner than to the sinned against.

Chapter 18. —It is Never Allowable to Tell a Lie; But Lies Differ Very Much in Guilt, According to the Intention and the Subject.

But here arises a very difficult and very intricate question, about which I once wrote a large book, finding it necessary to give it an answer. The question is this: whether at any time it can become the duty of a good man to tell a lie? For some go so far as to contend that there are occasions on which it is a good and pious work to commit perjury even, and to say what is false about matters that relate to the worship of God, and about the very nature of God Himself. To me, however, it seems certain that every lie is a sin, though it makes a great difference with what intention and on what subject one lies. For the sin of the man who tells a lie to help another is not so heinous as that of the man who tells a lie to injure another; and the man who by his lying puts a traveler on the wrong road, does not do so much harm as the man who by false or misleading representations distorts the whole course of a life. No one, of course, is to be condemned as a liar who says what is false, believing it to be true, because such a one does not consciously deceive, but rather is himself deceived. And, on the same principle, a man is not to be accused of lying, though he may sometimes be open to the charge of rashness, if through carelessness he takes up what is false and holds it as true; but, on the other hand, the man who says what is true, believing it to be false, is, so far as his own consciousness is concerned, a liar. For in saying what he does not believe, he says what to his own conscience is false, even though it should in fact be true; nor is the man in any sense free from lying who with his mouth speaks the truth without knowing it, but in his heart wills to tell a lie. And, therefore, not looking at the matter spoken of, but solely at the intention of the speaker, the man who unwittingly says what is false, thinking all the time that it is true, is a better man than the one who unwittingly says what is true, but in his conscience intends to deceive. For the former does not think one thing and say another; but the latter, though his statements may be true in fact, has one thought in his heart and another on his lips: and that is the very essence of lying. But when we come to consider truth and falsehood in respect to the subjects spoken of, the point on which one deceives or is deceived becomes a matter of the utmost importance. For although, as far as a man's own conscience is concerned, it is a greater evil to deceive than to be deceived, nevertheless it is a far less evil to tell a lie regarding matters that do not relate to religion, than to be led into error regarding matters the knowledge and belief of which are essential to the right worship of God. To illustrate this by example: suppose that one man should say of someone who is dead that he is still alive, knowing this to be untrue; and that another man should, being deceived, believe that Christ shall at the end of sometime (make the time as long as you please) die; would it not be incomparably better to lie like the former, than to be deceived like the latter? and would it not be a much less evil to lead some man into the former error, than to be led by any man into the latter?

Chapter 19. —Men's Errors Vary Very Much in the Magnitude of the Evils They Produce; But Yet Every Error is in Itself an Evil.

In some things, then, it is a great evil to be deceived; in some it is a small evil; in some no evil at all; and in some it is an actual advantage. It is to his grievous injury that a man is deceived when he does not believe what leads to eternal life, or believes what leads to eternal death. It is a small evil for a man to be deceived, when, by taking falsehood for truth, he brings upon himself temporal annoyances; for the patience of the believer will turn even these to a good use, as when, for example, taking a bad man for a good, he receives injury from him. But one who believes a bad man to be good, and yet suffers no injury, is nothing the worse for being deceived, nor does he fall under the prophetic denunciation: "Woe to those who call evil good!" For we are to understand that this is spoken not about evil men, but about the things that make men evil. Hence the man who calls adultery good, falls justly under that prophetic denunciation. But the man who calls the adulterer good, thinking him to be chaste, and not knowing him to be an adulterer, falls into no error regarding the nature of good and evil, but only makes a mistake as to the secrets of human conduct. He calls the man good on the ground of believing him to be what is undoubtedly good; he calls the adulterer evil, and the pure man good; and he calls this man good, not knowing him to be an adulterer, but believing him to be pure. Further, if by making a mistake one escape death, as I have said above once happened to me, one even derives some advantage from one's mistake. But when I assert that in certain cases a man may be deceived without any injury to himself, or even with some advantage to himself, I do not mean that the mistake in itself is no evil, or is in any sense a good; I refer only to the evil that is avoided, or the advantage that is gained, through making the mistake. For the mistake, considered in itself, is an evil: a great evil if it concern a great matter, a small evil if it concern a small matter, but yet always an evil. For who that is of sound mind can deny that it is an evil to receive what is false as if it were true, and to reject what is true as if it were false, or to hold what is uncertain as certain, and what is certain as uncertain? But it is one thing to think a man good when he is really bad, which is a mistake; it is another thing to suffer no ulterior injury in consequence of the mistake, supposing that the bad man whom we think good inflicts no damage upon us. In the same way, it is one thing to think that we are on the right road when we are not; it is another thing when this mistake of ours, which is an evil, leads to some good, such as saving us from an ambush of wicked men.

Chapter 20. —Every Error is Not a Sin. An Examination of the Opinion of the Academic Philosophers, that to Avoid Error We Should in All Cases Suspend Belief.

I am not sure whether mistakes such as the following,—when one forms a good opinion of a bad man, not knowing what sort of man he is; or when, instead of the ordinary perceptions through the bodily senses, other appearances of a similar kind present themselves, which we perceive in the spirit, but think we perceive in the body, or perceive in the body, but think we perceive in the spirit (such a mistake as the Apostle Peter made when the angel suddenly freed him from his chains and imprisonment, and he thought he saw a vision); or when, in the case of sensible objects themselves, we mistake rough for smooth, or bitter for sweet, or think that putrid matter has a good smell; or when we mistake the passing of a carriage for thunder; or mistake one man for another, the two being very much alike, as often happens in the case of twins (hence our great poet calls it "a mistake pleasing to parents"),—whether these, and other mistakes of this kind, ought to be called sins. Nor do I now undertake to solve a very knotty question, which perplexed those very acute thinkers, the Academic philosophers: whether a wise man ought to give his assent to anything, seeing that he may fall into error by assenting to falsehood: for all things, as they assert, are either unknown or uncertain. Now I wrote three volumes shortly after my conversion, to remove out of my way the objections which lie, as it were, on the very threshold of faith. And assuredly it was necessary at the very outset to remove this utter despair of reaching truth, which seems to be strengthened by the arguments of these philosophers. Now in their eyes every error is regarded as a sin, and they think that error can only be avoided by entirely suspending belief. For they say that the man who assents to what is uncertain falls into error; and they strive by the most acute, but most audacious arguments, to show that, even though a man's opinion should by chance be true, yet that there is no certainty of its truth, owing to the impossibility of distinguishing truth from falsehood. But with us, "the just shall live by faith." Now, if assent be taken away, faith goes too; for without assent there can be no belief. And there are truths, whether we know them or not, which must be believed if we would attain to a happy life, that is, to eternal life. But I am not sure whether one ought to argue with men who not only do not know that there is an eternal life before them, but do not know whether they are living at the present moment; nay, say that they do not know what it is impossible they can be ignorant of. For it is impossible that anyone should be ignorant that he is alive, seeing that if he be not alive it is impossible for him to be ignorant; for not knowledge merely, but ignorance too, can be an attribute only of the living. But, forsooth, they think that by not acknowledging that they are alive they avoid error, when even their very error proves that they are alive, since one who is not alive cannot err. As, then, it is not only true, but certain, that we are alive, so there are many other things both true and certain; and God forbid that it should ever be called wisdom, and not the height of folly, to refuse assent to these.

Chapter 21. —Error, Though Not Always a Sin, is Always an Evil.

But as to those matters regarding which our belief or disbelief, and indeed their truth or supposed truth or falsity, are of no importance whatever, so far as attaining the kingdom of God is concerned: to make a mistake in such matters is not to be looked on as a sin, or at least as a very small and trifling sin. In short, a mistake in matters of this kind, whatever its nature and magnitude, does not relate to the way of approach to God, which is the faith of Christ that "worketh by love." For the "mistake pleasing to parents" in the case of the twin children was no deviation from this way; nor did the Apostle Peter deviate from this way, when, thinking that he saw a vision, he so mistook one thing for another, that, till the angel who delivered him had departed from him, he did not distinguish the real objects among which he was moving from the visionary objects of a dream; nor did the patriarch Jacob deviate from this way, when he believed that his son, who was really alive, had been slain by a beast. In the case of these and other false impressions of the same kind, we are indeed deceived, but our faith in God remains secure. We go astray, but we do not leave the way that leads us to Him. But yet these errors, though they are not sinful, are to be reckoned among the evils of this life which is so far made subject to vanity, that we receive what is false as if it were true, reject what is true as if it were false, and cling to what is uncertain as if it were certain. And although they do not trench upon that true and certain faith through which we reach eternal blessedness, yet they have much to do with that misery in which we are now living. And assuredly, if we were now in the enjoyment of the true and perfect happiness that lies before us, we should not be subject to any deception through any sense, whether of body or of mind.

Chapter 22. —A Lie is Not Allowable, Even to Save Another from Injury.

But every lie must be called a sin, because not only when a man knows the truth, but even when, as a man may be, he is mistaken and deceived, it is his duty to say what he thinks in his heart, whether it be true, or whether he only think it to be true. But every liar says the opposite of what he thinks in his heart, with purpose to deceive. Now it is evident that speech was given to man, not that men might therewith deceive one another, but that one man might make known his thoughts to another. To use speech, then, for the purpose of deception, and not for its appointed end, is a sin. Nor are we to suppose that there is any lie that is not a sin, because it is sometimes possible, by telling a lie, to do service to another. For it is possible to do this by theft also, as when we steal from a rich man who never feels the loss, to give to a poor man who is sensibly benefited by what he gets. And the same can be said of adultery also, when, for instance, some woman appears likely to die of love unless we consent to her wishes, while if she lived she might purify herself by repentance; but yet no one will assert that on this account such an adultery is not a sin. And if we justly place so high a value upon chastity, what offense have we taken at truth, that, while no prospect of advantage to another will lead us to violate the former by adultery, we should be ready to violate the latter by lying? It cannot be denied that they have attained a very high standard of goodness who never lie except to save a man from injury; but in the case of men who have reached this standard, it is not the deceit, but their good intention, that is justly praised, and sometimes even rewarded. It is quite enough that the deception should be pardoned, without its being made an object of laudation, especially among the heirs of the new covenant, to whom it is said: "Let your communication be, Yea, yea; Nay, nay: for whatsoever is more than these cometh of evil." And it is because this evil, which never ceases to creep in while we retain this mortal vesture, that the co-heirs of Christ themselves say, "Forgive us our debts."

Chapter 23. —Summary of the Results of the Preceding Discussion.

As it is right that we should know the causes of good and evil, so much of them at least as will suffice for the way that leads us to the kingdom, where there will be life without the shadow of death, truth without any alloy of error, and happiness unbroken by any sorrow, I have discussed these subjects with the brevity which my limited space demanded. And I think there cannot now be any doubt, that the only cause of any good that we enjoy is the goodness of God, and that the only cause of evil is the falling away from the unchangeable good of a being made good but changeable, first in the case of an angel, and afterwards in the case of man.

Chapter 24. —The Secondary Causes of Evil are Ignorance and Lust.

This is the first evil that befell the intelligent creation—that is, its first privation of good. Following upon this crept in, and now even in opposition to man's will, ignorance of duty, and lust after what is hurtful: and these brought in their train error and suffering, which, when they are felt to be imminent, produce that shrinking of the mind which is called fear. Further, when the mind attains the objects of its desire, however hurtful or empty they may be, error prevents it from perceiving their true nature, or its perceptions are overborne by a diseased appetite, and so it is puffed up with a foolish joy. From these fountains of evil, which spring out of defect rather than superfluity, flows every form of misery that besets a rational nature.

Chapter 25. —God's Judgments Upon Fallen Men and Angels. The Death of the Body is Man's Peculiar Punishment.

And yet such a nature, in the midst of all its evils, could not lose the craving after happiness. Now the evils I have mentioned are common to all who for their wickedness have been justly condemned by God, whether they be men or angels. But there is one form of punishment peculiar to man—the death of the body. God had threatened him with this punishment of death if he should sin, leaving him indeed to the freedom of his own will, but yet commanding his obedience under pain of death; and He placed him amid the happiness of Eden, as it were in a protected nook of life, with the intention that, if he preserved his righteousness, he should thence ascend to a better place.

Chapter 26. —Through Adam's Sin His Whole Posterity Were Corrupted, and Were Born Under the Penalty of Death, Which He Had Incurred.

Thence, after his sin, he was driven into exile, and by

his sin the whole race of which he was the root was corrupted in him, and thereby subjected to the penalty of death. And so it happens that all descended from him, and from the woman who had led him into sin, and was condemned at the same time with him, —being the offspring of carnal lust on which the same punishment of disobedience was visited, —were tainted with the original sin, and were by it drawn through divers errors and sufferings into that last and endless punishment which they suffer in common with the fallen angels, their corrupters and masters, and the partakers of their doom. And thus "by one man sin entered into the world, and death by sin; and so death passed upon all men, for that all have sinned." By "the world" the apostle, of course, means in this place the whole human race.

Chapter 27. —The State of Misery to Which Adam's Sin Reduced Mankind, and the Restoration Effected Through the Mercy of God.

Thus, then, matters stood. The whole mass of the human race was under condemnation, was lying steeped and wallowing in misery, and was being tossed from one form of evil to another, and, having joined the faction of the fallen angels, was paying the well-merited penalty of that impious rebellion. For whatever the wicked freely do through blind and unbridled lust, and whatever they suffer against their will in the way of open punishment, this all evidently pertains to the just wrath of God. But the goodness of the Creator never fails either to supply life and vital power to the wicked angels (without which their existence would soon come to an end); or, in the case of mankind, who spring from a condemned and corrupt stock, to impart form and life to their seed, to fashion their members, and through the various seasons of their life, and in the different parts of the earth, to quicken their senses, and bestow upon them the nourishment they need. For He judged it better to bring good out of evil, than not to permit any evil to exist. And if He had determined that in the case of men, as in the case of the fallen angels, there should be no restoration to happiness, would it not have been quite just, that the being who rebelled against God, who in the abuse of his freedom spurned and transgressed the command of his Creator when he could so easily have kept it, who defaced in himself the image of his Creator by stubbornly turning away from His light, who by an evil use of his free-will broke away from his wholesome bondage to the Creator's laws,—would it not have been just that such a being should have been wholly and to all eternity deserted by God, and left to suffer the everlasting punishment he had so richly earned? Certainly, so God would have done, had He been only just and not also merciful, and had He not designed that His unmerited mercy should shine forth the more brightly in contrast with the unworthiness of its objects.

Chapter 28. —When the Rebellious Angels Were Cast Out, the Rest Remained in the Enjoyment of Eternal Happiness with God.

Whilst some of the angels, then, in their pride and impiety rebelled against God, and were cast down from their heavenly abode into the lowest darkness, the remaining number dwelt with God in eternal and unchanging purity and happiness. For all were not sprung from one angel who had fallen and been condemned, so that they were not all, like men, involved by one original sin in the bonds of an inherited guilt, and so made subject to the penalty which one had incurred; but when he, who afterwards became the devil, was with his associates in crime exalted in pride, and by that very exaltation was with them cast down, the rest remained steadfast in piety and obedience to their Lord, and obtained, what before they had not enjoyed, a sure and certain knowledge of their eternal safety, and freedom from the possibility of falling.

Chapter 29. —The Restored Part of Humanity Shall, in Accordance with the Promises of God, Succeed to the Place Which the Rebellious Angels Lost.

And so it pleased God, the Creator and Governor of the universe, that, since the whole body of the angels had not fallen into rebellion, the part of them which had fallen should remain in perdition eternally, and that the other part, which had in the rebellion remained steadfastly loyal, should rejoice in the sure and certain knowledge of their eternal happiness; but that, on the other hand, mankind, who constituted the remainder of the intelligent creation, having perished without exception under sin, both original and actual, and the consequent punishments, should be in part restored, and should fill up the gap which the rebellion and fall of the devils had left in the company of the angels. For this is the promise to the saints, that at the resurrection they shall be equal to the angels of God. And thus, the Jerusalem which is above, which is the mother of us all, the city of God, shall not be spoiled of any of the number of her citizens, shall perhaps reign over even a more abundant population. We do not know the number either of the saints or of the devils; but we know that the children of the holy mother who was called barren on earth shall succeed to the place of the fallen angels, and shall dwell forever in that peaceful abode from which they fell. But the number of the citizens, whether as it now is or as it shall be, is present to the thoughts of the great Creator, who calls those things which are not as though they were, and ordered all things in measure, and number, and weight.

Chapter 30. —Men are Not Saved by Good Works, Nor by the Free Determination of Their Own Will, But by the Grace of God Through Faith.

But this part of the human race to which God has promised pardon and a share in His eternal kingdom, can they be restored through the merit of their own works? God forbid. For what good work can a lost man perform, except so far as he has been delivered from perdition? Can they do anything by the free determination of their own will? Again I say, God forbid. For it was by the evil use of his free-will that man destroyed both it and himself. For, as a man who kills himself must, of course, be alive when he kills himself, but after he has killed himself ceases to live, and cannot restore himself to life; so, when man by his own free-will sinned, then sin being victorious over him, the freedom of his will was lost. "For of whom a man is overcome, of the same is he brought in bondage." This is the judgment of the Apostle Peter. And as it is certainly true, what kind of liberty, I ask, can the bondslave possess, except when it pleases him to sin? For he is freely in bondage who does with pleasure the will of his master. Accordingly, he who is the servant of sin is free to sin. And hence he will not be free to do right, until, being freed from sin, he shall begin to be the servant of righteousness. And this is true liberty, for he has pleasure in the righteous deed; and it is at the same time a holy bondage, for he is obedient to the will of God. But whence comes this liberty to do right to the man who is in bondage and sold under sin, except he be redeemed by Him who has said, "If the Son shall make you free, ye shall be free indeed?" And before this redemption is wrought in a man, when he is not yet free to do what is right, how can he talk of the freedom of his will and his good works, except he be inflated by that foolish pride of boasting which the apostle restrains when he says, "By grace are ye saved, through faith."

Chapter 31. —Faith Itself is the Gift of God; And Good Works Will Not Be Wanting in Those Who Believe.

And lest men should arrogate to themselves the merit of their own faith at least, not understanding that this too is the gift of God, this same apostle, who says in another place that he had "obtained mercy of the Lord to be faithful," here also adds: "and that not of yourselves; it is the gift of God: not of works, lest any man should boast." And lest it should be thought that good works will be wanting in those who believe, he adds further: "For we are His workmanship, created in Christ Jesus unto good works, which God hath before ordained that we should walk in them." We shall be made truly free, then, when God fashions us, that is, forms and creates us anew, not as men—for He has done that already—but as good men, which His grace is now doing, that we may be a new creation in Christ Jesus, according as it is said: "Create in me a clean heart, O God." For God had already created his heart, so far as the physical structure of the human heart is concerned; but the psalmist prays for the renewal of the life which was still lingering in his heart.

Chapter 32. —The Freedom of the Will is Also the Gift of God, for God Worketh in Us Both to Will and to Do.

And further, should anyone be inclined to boast, not indeed of his works, but of the freedom of his will, as if the first merit belonged to him, this very liberty of good action being given to him as a reward he had earned, let him listen to this same preacher of grace, when he says: "For it is God which worketh in you, both to will and to do of His own good pleasure;" and in another place: "So, then, it is not of him that willeth, nor of him that runneth, but of God that showed mercy." Now as, undoubtedly, if a man is of the age to use his reason, he cannot believe, hope, love, unless he will to do so, nor obtain the prize of the high calling of God unless he voluntarily run for it; in what sense is it "not of him that willeth, nor of him that runneth, but of God that showed mercy," except that, as it is written, "the preparation of the heart is from the Lord?" Otherwise, if it is said, "It is not of him that willeth, nor of him that runneth, but of God that showed mercy," because it is of both, that is, both of the will of man and of the mercy of God, so that we are to understand the saying, "It is not of him that willeth, nor of him that runneth, but of God that showed mercy," as if it meant the will of man alone is not sufficient, if the mercy of God go not with it,—then it will follow that the mercy of God alone is not sufficient, if the will of man go not with it; and therefore, if we may rightly say, "it is not of man that willeth, but of God that showed mercy," because the will of man by itself is not enough, why may we not also rightly put it in the converse way: "It is not of God that showed mercy, but of man that willeth," because the mercy of God by itself does not suffice? Surely, if no Christian will dare to say this, "It is not of God that showed mercy, but of man that willeth," lest he should openly contradict the apostle, it follows that the true interpretation of the saying, "It is not of him that willeth, nor of him that runneth, but of God that showed mercy," is that the whole work belongs to God, who both makes the will of man righteous, and thus prepares it for assistance, and assists it when it is prepared. For the man's righteousness of will precedes many of God's gifts, but not all; and it must itself be included among those which it does not precede. We read in Holy Scripture, both that God's mercy "shall meet me," and that His mercy "shall follow me." It goes before the unwilling to make him willing; it follows the willing to make his will effectual. Why are we taught to pray for our enemies, who are plainly unwilling to lead a holy life, unless that God may work willingness in them? And why are we ourselves taught to ask that we may receive, unless that He who has created in us the wish, may Himself satisfy the wish? We pray, then, for our enemies, that the mercy of God may prevent them, as it has prevented us: we pray for ourselves that His mercy may follow us.

Chapter 33. —Men, Being by Nature the Children of Wrath, Needed a Mediator. In What Sense God is Said to Be Angry.

And so, the human race was lying under a just condemnation, and all men were the children of wrath. Of which wrath it is written: "All our days are passed away in Thy wrath; we spend our years as a tale that is told." Of which wrath also Job says: "Man that is born of a woman is of few days, and full of trouble." Of which wrath also the Lord Jesus says: "He that believeth on the Son hath everlasting life: and he that believeth not the Son shall not see life; but the wrath of God abided on him." He does not say it will come, but it "abided on him." For every man is born with it; wherefore the apostle says: "We were by nature the children of wrath, even as others." Now, as men were lying under this wrath because of their original sin, and as this original sin was the more heavy and deadly in proportion to the number and magnitude of the actual sins which were added to it, there was need for a Mediator, that is, for a reconciler, who, by the offering of one sacrifice, of which all the sacrifices of the law and the prophets were types, should take away this wrath. Wherefore the apostle says: "For if, when we were enemies, we were reconciled to God by the death of His Son, much more, being reconciled, we shall be saved by His life." Now when God is said to be angry, we do not attribute to Him such a disturbed feeling as exists in the mind of an angry man; but we call His just displeasure against sin by the name "anger," a word transferred by analogy from human emotions. But our being reconciled to God through a Mediator, and receiving the Holy Spirit, so that we who were enemies are made sons ("For as many as are led by the Spirit of God, they are the sons of God"): this is the grace of God through Jesus Christ our Lord.

Chapter 34. —The Ineffable Mystery of the Birth of Christ the Mediator Through the Virgin Mary.

Now of this Mediator it would occupy too much space to say anything at all worthy of Him; and, indeed, to say what is worthy of Him is not in the power of man. For who will explain in consistent words this single statement, that "the Word was made flesh, and dwelt among us," so that we may believe on the only Son of God the Father Almighty, born of the Holy Ghost and the Virgin Mary. The meaning of the Word being made flesh, is not that the divine nature was changed into flesh, but that the divine nature assumed our flesh. And by "flesh" we are here to understand "man," the part being put for the whole, as when it is said: "By the deeds of the law shall no flesh be justified," that is, no man. For we must believe that no part was wanting in that human nature which He put on, save that it was a nature wholly free from every taint of sin, —not such a nature as is conceived between the two sexes through carnal lust, which is born in sin, and whose guilt is washed away in regeneration; but such as it behooved a virgin to bring forth, when the mother's faith, not her lust, was the condition of conception. And if her virginity had been marred even in bringing Him forth, He would not have been born of a virgin; and it would be false (which God forbid) that He was born of the Virgin Mary, as is believed and declared by the whole Church, which, in imitation of His mother, daily brings forth members of His body, and yet remains a virgin. Read, if you please, my letter on the virginity of the holy Mary which I sent to that eminent man, whose name I mention with respect and affection, Volusianus.

Chapter 35. —Jesus Christ, Being the Only Son of God, is at the Same Time Man.

Wherefore Christ Jesus, the Son of God, is both God and man; God before all worlds; man in our world: God, because the Word of God (for "the Word was God"); and man, because in His one person the Word was joined with a body and a rational soul. Wherefore, so far as He is God, He and the Father are one; so far as He is man, the Father is greater than He. For when He was the only Son of God, not by grace, but by nature, that He might be also full of grace, He became the Son of man; and He Himself unites both natures in His own identity, and both natures constitute one Christ; because, "being in the form of God, He thought it not robbery to be," what He was by nature, "equal with God." But He made Himself of no reputation, and took upon Himself the form of a servant, not losing or lessening the form of God. And, accordingly, He was both made less and remained equal, being both in one, as has been said: but He was one of these as Word, and the other as man. As Word, He is equal with the Father; as man, less than the Father. One Son of God, and at the same time Son of man; one Son of man, and at the same time Son of God; not two Sons of

God, God and man, but one Son of God: God without beginning; man with a beginning, our Lord Jesus Christ.

Chapter 36. —The Grace of God is Clearly and Remarkably Displayed in Raising the Man Christ Jesus to the Dignity of the Son of God.

Now here the grace of God is displayed with the greatest power and clearness. For what merit had the human nature in the man Christ earned, that it should in this unparalleled way be taken up into the unity of the person of the only Son of God? What goodness of will, what goodness of desire and intention, what good works, had gone before, which made this man worthy to become one person with God? Had He been a man previously to this, and had He earned this unprecedented reward, that He should be thought worthy to become God? Assuredly nay; from the very moment that He began to be man, He was nothing else than the Son of God, the only Son of God, the Word who was made flesh, and therefore He was God so that just as each individual man unites in one person a body and a rational soul, so Christ in one person unites the Word and man. Now wherefore was this unheard of glory conferred on human nature, —a glory which, as there was no antecedent merit, was of course wholly of grace, —except that here those who looked at the matter soberly and honestly might behold a clear manifestation of the power of God's free grace, and might understand that they are justified from their sins by the same grace which made the man Christ Jesus free from the possibility of sin? And so the angel, when he announced to Christ's mother the coming birth, saluted her thus: "Hail, thou that art full of grace;" and shortly afterwards, "Thou hast found grace with God." Now she was said to be full of grace, and to have found grace with God, because she was to be the mother of her Lord, nay, of the Lord of all flesh. But, speaking of Christ Himself, the evangelist John, after saying, "The Word was made flesh, and dwelt among us," adds, "and we beheld His glory, the glory as of the only-begotten of the Father, full of grace and truth." When he says, "The Word was made flesh," this is "full of grace;" when he says, "the glory of the only-begotten of the Father," this is "full of truth." For the Truth Himself, who was the only-begotten of the Father, not by grace, but by nature, by grace took our humanity upon Him, and so united it with His own person that He Himself became also the Son of man.

Chapter 37. —The Same Grace is Further Clearly Manifested in This, that the Birth of Christ According to the Flesh is of the Holy Ghost.

For the same Jesus Christ who is the only-begotten, that is, the only Son of God, our Lord, was born of the Holy Ghost and of the Virgin Mary. And we know that the Holy Spirit is the gift of God, the gift being Himself indeed equal to the Giver. And therefore, the Holy Spirit also is God, not inferior to the Father and the Son. The fact, therefore, that the nativity of Christ in His human nature was by the Holy Spirit, is another clear manifestation of grace. For when the Virgin asked the angel how this which he had announced should be, seeing she knew not a man, the angel answered, "The Holy Ghost shall come upon thee, and the power of the Highest shall overshadow thee: therefore also that holy thing which shall be born of thee shall be called the Son of God." And when Joseph was minded to put her away, suspecting her of adultery, as he knew she was not with child by himself, he was told by the angel, "Fear not to take unto thee Mary thy wife; for that which is conceived in her is of the Holy Ghost:" that is, what thou suspectest to be begotten of another man is of the Holy Ghost.

Chapter 38. —Jesus Christ, According to the Flesh, Was Not Born of the Holy Spirit in Such a Sense that the Holy Spirit is His Father.

Nevertheless, are we on this account to say that the Holy Ghost is the father of the man Christ, and that as God the Father begat the Word, so God the Holy Spirit begat the man, and that these two natures constitute the one Christ; and that as the Word He is the Son of God the Father, and as man the Son of God the Holy Spirit, because the Holy Spirit as His father begat Him of the Virgin Mary? Who will dare to say so? Nor is it necessary to show by reasoning how many other absurdities flow from this supposition, when it is itself so absurd that no believer's ears can bear to hear it. Hence, as we confess, "Our Lord Jesus Christ, who of God is God, and as man was born of the Holy Ghost and of the Virgin Mary, having both natures, the divine and the human, is the only Son of God the Father Almighty, from whom proceeded the Holy Spirit." Now in what sense do we say that Christ was born of the Holy Spirit, if the Holy Spirit did not beget Him? Is it that He made Him, since our Lord Jesus Christ, though as God "all things were made by Him," yet as man was Himself made; as the apostle says, "who was made of the seed of David according to the flesh?" But as that created thing which the Virgin conceived and brought forth though it was united only to the person of the Son, was made by the whole Trinity (for the works of the Trinity are not separable), why should the Holy Spirit alone be mentioned as having made it? Or is it that, when one of the Three is mentioned as the author of any work, the whole Trinity is to be understood as working? That is true, and can be proved by examples. But we need not dwell longer on this solution. For the puzzle is, in what sense it is said, "born of the Holy Ghost," when He is in no sense the Son of the Holy Ghost? For though God made this world, it would not be right to say that it is the Son of God, or that it was born of God; we would say that it was created, or made, or framed, or ordered by Him, or whatever form of expression we can properly use. Here, then, when we make confession that Christ was born of the Holy Ghost and of the Virgin Mary, it is difficult to explain how it is that He is not the Son of the Holy Ghost and is the Son of the Virgin Mary, when He was born both of Him and of her. It is clear beyond a doubt that He was not born of the Holy Spirit as His father, in the same sense that He was born of the Virgin as His mother.

Chapter 39. —Not Everything that is Born of Another is to Be Called a Son of that Other.

We need not therefore take for granted, that whatever is born of a thing is forthwith to be declared the son of that thing. For, to pass over the fact that a son is born of a man in a different sense from that in which a hair or a louse is born of him, neither of these being a son; to pass over this, I say, as too mean an illustration for a subject of so much importance: it is certain that those who are born of water and of the Holy Spirit cannot with propriety be called sons of the water though they are called sons of God the Father, and of the Church their mother. In the same way, then, He who was born of the Holy Spirit is the Son of God the Father, not of the Holy Spirit. For what I have said of the hair and the other things is sufficient to show us that not everything which is born of another can be called the son of that of which it is born, just as it does not follow that all who are called a man's sons were born of him, for some sons are adopted. And some men are called sons of hell, not as being born of hell, but as prepared for it, as the sons of the kingdom are prepared for the kingdom.

Chapter 40. —Christ's Birth Through the Holy Spirit Manifests to Us the Grace of God.

And, therefore, as one thing may be born of another, and yet not in such a way as to be its son, and as not everyone who is called a son was born of him whose son he is called, it is clear that this arrangement by which Christ was born of the Holy Spirit, but not as His son, and of the Virgin Mary as her son, is intended as a manifestation of the grace of God. For it was by this grace that a man, without any antecedent merit, was at the very commencement of His existence as man, so united in one person with the Word of God, that the very person who was Son of man was at the same time Son of God, and the very person who was Son of God was at the same time Son of man; and in the adoption of His human nature into the divine, the grace itself became in a way so natural to the man, as to leave no room for the entrance of sin. Wherefore this grace is signified by the Holy Spirit; for He, though in His own nature God, may also be called the gift of God. And to explain all this sufficiently, if indeed it could be done at all, would require a very lengthened discussion.

Chapter 41. —Christ, Who Was Himself Free from Sin, Was Made Sin for Us, that We Might Be Reconciled to God.

Begotten and conceived, then, without any indulgence of carnal lust, and therefore bringing with Him no original sin, and by the grace of God joined and united in a wonderful and unspeakable way in one person with the Word, the Only-begotten of the Father, a son by nature, not by grace, and therefore having no sin of His own; nevertheless, because the likeness of sinful flesh in which He came, He was called sin, that He might be sacrificed to wash away sin. For, under the Old Covenant, sacrifices for sin were called sins. And He, of whom all these sacrifices were types and shadows, was Himself truly made sin. Hence the apostle, after saying, "We pray you in Christ's stead, be ye reconciled to God," forthwith adds: "for He hath made Him to be sin for us who knew no sin; that we might be made the righteousness of God in Him." He does not say, as some incorrect copies read, "He who knew no sin did sin for us," as if Christ had Himself sinned for our sakes; but he says, "Him who knew no sin," that is, Christ, God, to whom we are to be reconciled, "hath made to be sin for us," that is, hath made Him a sacrifice for our sins, by which we might be reconciled to God. He, then, being made sin, just as we are made righteousness (our righteousness being not our own, but God's, not in ourselves, but in Him); He being made sin, not His own, but ours, not in Himself, but in us, showed, by the likeness of sinful flesh in which He was crucified, that though sin was not in Him, yet that in a certain sense He died to sin, by dying in the flesh which was the likeness of sin; and that although He Himself had never lived the old life of sin, yet by His resurrection He typified our new life springing up out of the old death in sin.

Chapter 42. —The Sacrament of Baptism Indicates Our Death with Christ to Sin, and Our Resurrection with Him to Newness of Life.

And this is the meaning of the great sacrament of baptism which is solemnized among us, that all who attain to this grace should die to sin, as He is said to have died to sin, because He died in the flesh, which is the likeness of sin; and rising from the font regenerate, as He arose alive from the grave, should begin a new life in the Spirit, whatever may be the age of the body?

Chapter 43. —Baptism and the Grace Which It Typifies are Open to All, Both Infants and Adults.

For from the infant newly born to the old man bent with age, as there is none shut out from baptism, so there is none who in baptism does not die to sin. But infants die only to original sin; those who are older die also to all the sins which their evil lives have added to the sin which they brought with them.

Chapter 44. —In Speaking of Sin, the Singular Number is Often Put for the Plural, and the Plural for the Singular.

But even these latter are frequently said to die to sin, though undoubtedly they die not to one sin, but to all the numerous actual sins they have committed in thought, word, or deed: for the singular number is often put for the plural, as when the poet says, "They fill its belly with the armed soldier," though in the case here referred to there were many soldiers concerned. And we read in our own Scriptures: "Pray to the Lord, that He take away the serpent from us." He does not say serpents though the people were suffering from many; and so in other cases. When, on the other hand, the original sin is expressed in the plural number, as when we say that infants are baptized for the remission of sins, instead of saying for the remission of sin, this is the converse figure of speech, by which the plural number is put in place of the singular; as in the Gospel it is said of the death of Herod, "for they are dead which sought the young child's life," instead of saying, "he is dead." And in Exodus: "They have made them," Moses says, "gods of gold," though they had made only one calf, of which they said: "These be thy gods, O Israel, which brought thee up out of the land of Egypt,"—here, too, putting the plural in place of the singular.

Chapter 45. —In Adam's First Sin, Many Kinds of Sin Were Involved.

However, even in that one sin, which "by one man entered into the world, and so passed upon all men," and because which infants are baptized, a number of distinct sins may be observed, if it be analyzed as it were into its separate elements. For there is in it pride, because man chose to be under his own dominion, rather than under the dominion of God; and blasphemy, because he did not believe God; and murder, for he brought death upon himself; and spiritual fornication, for the purity of the human soul was corrupted by the seducing blandishments of the serpent; and theft, for man turned to his own use the food he had been forbidden to touch; and avarice, for he had a craving for more than should have been sufficient for him; and whatever other sin can be discovered on careful reflection to be involved in this one admitted sin.

Chapter 46. —It is Probable that Children are Involved in the Guilt Not Only of the First Pair, But of Their Own Immediate Parents.

And it is said, with much appearance of probability, that infants are involved in the guilt of the sins not only of the first pair, but of their own immediate parents. For that divine judgment, "I shall visit the iniquities of the fathers upon the children," certainly applies to them before they come under the new covenant by regeneration. And it was this new covenant that was prophesied of, when it was said by Ezekiel, that the sons should not bear the iniquity of the fathers, and that it should no longer be a proverb in Israel, "The fathers have eaten sour grapes, and the children's teeth are set on edge." Here lies the necessity that each man should be born again, that he might be freed from the sin in which he was born. For the sins committed afterwards can be cured by penitence, as we see is the case after baptism. And therefore the new birth would not have been appointed only that the first birth was sinful, so sinful that even one who was legitimately born in wedlock says: "I was shapen in iniquities, and in sins did my mother conceive me." He did not say in iniquity, or in sin, though he might have said so correctly; but he preferred to say "iniquities" and "sins," because in that one sin which passed upon all men, and which was so great that human nature was by it made subject to inevitable death, many sins, as I showed above, may be discriminated; and further, because there are other sins of the immediate parents, which though they have not the same effect in producing a change of nature, yet subject the children to guilt unless the divine grace and mercy interpose to rescue them.

Chapter 47. —It is Difficult to Decide Whether the Sins of a Man's Other Progenitors are Imputed to Him.

But about the sins of the other progenitors who intervene between Adam and a man's own parents, a question may very well be raised. Whether everyone who is born is involved in all their accumulated evil acts, in all their multiplied original guilt, so that the later he is born, so much the worse is his condition; or whether God threatens to visit the iniquity of the fathers upon the children unto the third and fourth generations, because in His mercy He does not extend His wrath against the sins of the progenitors further than that, lest those who do not obtain the grace of regeneration might be crushed down under too heavy a burden if they were compelled to bear as original guilt all the sins of all their progenitors from the very beginning of the human race, and to pay the penalty due to them; or whether any other solution of this great question may or may not be found in Scripture by a more diligent search and a more careful interpretation, I dare not rashly affirm.

Chapter 48. —The Guilt of the First Sin is So Great that It Can Be Washed Away Only in the Blood of the Mediator, Jesus Christ.

Nevertheless, that one sin, admitted into a place where such perfect happiness reigned, was of so heinous a character, that in one man the whole human race was originally, and as one may say, radically, condemned; and it cannot be pardoned and blotted out except through the one Mediator between God and men, the man Christ Jesus, who only has had power to be so born as not to need a second birth.

Chapter 49. —Christ Was Not Regenerated in the Baptism of John, But Submitted to It to Give Us an Example of Humility, Just as He Submitted to Death, Not as the Punishment of Sin, But to Take Away the Sin of the World.

Now, those who were baptized in the baptism of John, by whom Christ was Himself baptized, were not regenerated; but they were prepared through the ministry of His forerunner, who cried, "Prepare ye the way of the Lord," for Him in whom only they could be regenerated. For His baptism is not with water only, as was that of John, but with the Holy Ghost also; so that whoever believes in Christ is regenerated by that Spirit, of whom Christ being generated, He did not need regeneration. Whence that announcement of the Father which was heard after His baptism, "This day have I begotten Thee," referred not to that one day of time on which He was baptized, but to the one day of an unchangeable eternity, so as to show that this man was one in person with the Only-begotten. For when a day neither begins with the close of yesterday, nor ends with the beginning of to-morrow, it is an eternal to-day. Therefore, He asked to be baptized in water by John, not that any iniquity of His might be washed away, but that He might manifest the depth of His humility. For baptism found in Him nothing to wash away, as death found in Him nothing to punish; so that it was in the strictest justice, and not by the mere violence of power, that the devil was crushed and conquered: for, as he had most unjustly put Christ to death, though there was no sin in Him to deserve death, it was most just that through Christ he should lose his hold of those who by sin were justly subject to the bondage in which he held them. Both of these, then, that is, both baptism and death, were submitted to by Him, not through a pitiable necessity, but of His own free pity for us, and as part of an arrangement by which, as one man brought sin into the world, that is, upon the whole human race, so one man was to take away the sin of the world.

Chapter 50. —Christ Took Away Not Only the One Original Sin, But All the Other Sins that Have Been Added to It.

With this difference: the first man brought one sin into the world, but this man took away not only that one sin, but all that He found added to it. Hence the apostle says: "And not as it was by one that sinned, so is the gift: for the judgment was by one to condemnation, but the free gift is of many offenses unto justification." For it is evident that the one sin which we bring with us by nature would, even if it stood alone, bring us under condemnation; but the free gift justifies man from many offenses: for each man, in addition to the one sin which, in common with all his kind, he brings with him by nature, has committed many sins that are strictly his own.

Chapter 51. —All Men Born of Adam are Under Condemnation, and Only If New Born in Christ are Freed from Condemnation.

But what he says a little after, "Therefore, as by the offense of one judgment came upon all men to condemnation; even so by the righteousness of one the free gift came upon all men unto justification of life," shows clearly enough that there is no one born of Adam but is subject to condemnation, and that no one, unless he be new born in Christ, is freed from condemnation.

Chapter 52. —In Baptism, which is the Similitude of the Death and Resurrection of Christ, All, Both Infants and Adults, Die to Sin that They May Walk in Newness of Life.

And after he has said as much about the condemnation through one man, and the free gift through one man, as he deemed sufficient for that part of his epistle, the apostle goes on to speak of the great mystery of holy baptism in the cross of Christ, and to clearly explain to us that baptism in Christ is nothing else than a similitude of the death of Christ, and that the death of Christ on the cross is nothing but a similitude of the pardon of sin: so that just as real as is His death, so real is the remission of our sins; and just as real as is His resurrection, so real is our justification. He says: "What shall we say, then? Shall we continue in sin, that grace may abound?" For he had said previously, "But where sin, abounded, grace did much more abound." And therefore, he proposes to himself the question, whether it would be right to continue in sin for the sake of the consequent abounding grace. But he answers, "God forbid;" and adds, "How shall we, that are dead to sin, live any longer therein?" Then, to show that we are dead to sin, "Know ye not," he says, "that so many of us as were baptized into Jesus Christ, were baptized into His death?" If, then, the fact that we were baptized into the death of Christ proves that we are dead to sin, it follows that even infants who are baptized into Christ die to sin, being baptized into His death. For there is no exception made: "So many of us as were baptized into Jesus Christ, were baptized into His death." And this is said to prove that we are dead to sin. Now, to what sin do infants die in their regeneration but that sin which they bring with them at birth? And therefore to these also applies what follows: "Therefore we are buried with Him by baptism into death; that, like as Christ was raised up from the dead by the glory of the Father, even so we also should walk in newness of life. For if we have been planted together in the likeness of His death, we shall be also in the likeness of His resurrection: knowing this, that our old man is crucified with Him, that the body of sin might be destroyed, that henceforth we should not serve sin. For he that is dead is freed from sin. Now if we be dead with Christ, we believe that we shall also live with Him: knowing that Christ, being raised from the dead, dieth no more; death hath no more dominion over Him. For in that He died, He died unto sin once; but in that He lives, He lives unto God. Likewise reckon ye also yourselves to be dead indeed unto sin, but alive unto God through Jesus Christ our Lord." Now he had commenced with proving that we must not continue in sin that grace may abound, and had said: "How shall we that are dead to sin live any longer therein?" And to show that we are dead to sin, he added: "Know ye not, that so many of us as were baptized into Jesus Christ, were baptized into His death?" And so he concludes this whole passage just as he began it. For he has brought in the death of Christ in such a way as to imply that Christ Himself also died to sin. To what sin did He die if not to the flesh, in which there was not sin, but the likeness of sin, and which was therefore called by the name of sin? To those who are baptized into the death of Christ, then, —and this class includes not adults only, but infants as well, —he says: "Likewise reckon ye also yourselves to be dead indeed unto sin, but alive unto God through Jesus Christ our Lord."

Chapter 53. —Christ's Cross and Burial, Resurrection, Ascension, and Sitting Down at the Right Hand of God, are Images of the Christian Life.

All the events, then, of Christ's crucifixion, of His burial, of His resurrection the third day, of His ascension into heaven, of His sitting down at the right hand of the Father, were so ordered, that the life which the Christian leads here might be modelled upon them, not merely in a mystical sense, but in reality. For about His crucifixion it is said: "They that are Christ's have crucified the flesh, with the affections and lusts." And about His burial: "We are buried with Him by baptism into death." About His resurrection: "That, like as Christ was raised up from the dead by the glory of the Father, even so we also should walk in newness of life." And about His ascension into heaven and sitting down at the right hand of the Father: "If ye then be risen with Christ, seek those things which are above, where Christ sitteth on the right hand of God. Set your affection on things above, not on things on the earth. For ye are dead, and your life is hid with Christ in God."

Chapter 54. —Christ's Second Coming Does Not Belong to the Past, But Will Take Place at the End of the World.

But what we believe as to Christ's action in the future, when He shall come from heaven to judge the quick and the dead, has no bearing upon the life which we now lead here; for it forms no part of what He did upon earth, but is part of what He shall do at the end of the world. And it is to this that the apostle refers in what immediately follows the passage quoted above: "When Christ, who is our life, shall appear, then shall ye also appear with Him in glory."

Chapter 55. —The Expression, "Christ Shall Judge the Quick and the Dead," May Be Understood in Either of Two Senses.

Now the expression, "to judge the quick and the dead," may be interpreted in two ways: either we may understand by the "quick" those who at His advent shall not yet have died, but whom He shall find alive in the flesh, and by the "dead" those who have departed from the body, or who shall have departed before His coming; or we may understand the "quick" to mean the righteous, and the "dead" the unrighteous; for the righteous shall be judged as well as others. Now the judgment of God is sometimes taken in a bad sense, as, for example, "They that have done evil unto the resurrection of judgment;" sometimes in a good sense, as, "Save me, O God, by Thy name, and judge me by Thy strength." This is easily understood when we consider that it is the judgment of God which separates the good from the evil, and sets the good at His right hand, that they may be delivered from evil, and not destroyed with the wicked; and it is for this reason that the Psalmist cried, "Judge me, O God," and then added, as if in explanation, "and distinguish my cause from that of an ungodly nation."

Chapter 56. —The Holy Spirit and the Church. The Church is the Temple of God.

And now, having spoken of Jesus Christ, the only Son of God, our Lord, with the brevity suitable to a confession of our faith, we go on to say that we believe also in the Holy Ghost, —thus completing the Trinity which constitutes the Godhead. Then we mention the Holy Church. And thus, we are made to understand that the intelligent creation, which constitutes the free Jerusalem, ought to be subordinate in the order of speech to the Creator, the Supreme Trinity: for all that is said of the man Christ Jesus has reference, of course, to the unity of the person of the Only-begotten. Therefore, the true order of the Creed demanded that the Church should be made subordinate to the Trinity, as the house to Him who dwells in it, the temple to God who occupies it, and the city to its builder. And we are here to understand the whole Church, not that part of it only which wanders as a stranger on the earth, praising the name of God from the rising of the sun to the going down of the same, and singing a new song of deliverance from its old captivity; but that part also which has always from its creation remained steadfast to God in heaven, and has never experienced the misery consequent upon a fall. This part is made up of the holy angels, who enjoy uninterrupted happiness; and (as it is bound to do) it renders assistance to the part which is still wandering among strangers: for these two parts shall be one in the fellowship of eternity, and now they are one in the bonds of love, the whole having been ordained for the worship of the one God. Wherefore, neither the whole Church, nor any part of it, has any desire to be worshipped instead of God, nor to be God to anyone who belongs to the temple of God—that temple which is built up of the saints who were created by the uncreated God. And therefore the Holy Spirit, if a creature, could not be the Creator, but would be a part of the intelligent creation. He would simply be the highest creature, and therefore would not be mentioned in the Creed before the Church; for He Himself would belong to the Church, to that part of it which is in the heavens. And He would not have a temple, for He Himself would be part of a temple. Now He has a temple, of which the apostle says: "Know ye not that your body is the temple of the Holy Ghost, which is in you, which ye have of God?" Of which body he says in another place: "Know ye not that your bodies are the members of Christ?" How, then, is He not God, seeing that He has a temple? and how can He be less than Christ, whose members are His temple? Nor has He one temple, and God another, seeing that the same apostle says: "Know ye not that ye are the temple of God?" and adds, as proof of this, "and that the Spirit of God dwelleth in you." God, then, dwells in His temple: not the Holy Spirit only, but the Father also, and the Son, who says of His own body, through which He was made Head of the Church upon earth ("that in all things He might have the pre-eminence):" "Destroy this temple, and in three days I will raise it up." The temple of God, then, that is, of the Supreme Trinity as a whole, is the Holy Church, embracing in its full extent both heaven and earth.

Chapter 57. —The Condition of the Church in Heaven.

But of that part of the Church which is in heaven what can we say, except that no wicked one is found in it, and that no one has fallen from it, or shall ever fall from it, since the time that "God spared not the angels that sinned," as the Apostle Peter writes, "but cast them down to hell, and delivered them into chains of darkness, to be reserved unto judgment?"

Chapter 58. —We Have No Certain Knowledge of the Organization of the Angelic Society.

Now, what the organization is of that supremely happy society in heaven: what the differences of rank are, which explain the fact that while all are called by the general name angels, as we read in the Epistle to the Hebrews, "but to which of the angels said God at any time, Sit on my right hand?" (this form of expression being evidently designed to embrace all the angels without exception), we yet find that there are some called archangels; and whether the archangels are the same as those called hosts, so that the expression, "Praise ye Him, all His angels: praise ye Him, all His hosts," is the same as if it had been said, "Praise ye Him, all His angels: praise ye Him, all His archangels;" and what are the various significations of those four names under which the apostle seems to embrace the whole heavenly company without exception, "whether they be thrones, or dominions, or principalities, or powers:"—let those who are able answer these questions, if they can also prove their answers to be true; but as for me, I confess my ignorance. I am not even certain upon this point: whether the sun, and the moon, and all the stars, do not form part of this same society, though many consider them merely luminous bodies, without either sensation or intelligence.

Chapter 59. —The Bodies Assumed by Angels Raise a Very Difficult, and Not Very Useful, Subject of Discussion.

Further, who will tell with what sort of bodies it was that the angels appeared to men, making themselves not only visible, but tangible; and again, how it is that, not through material bodies, but by spiritual power, they present visions not to the bodily eyes, but to the spiritual eyes of the mind, or speak something not into the ear from without, but from within the soul of the man, they themselves being stationed there too, as it is written in the prophet, "And the angel that spoke in me said unto me" (he does not say, "that spoke to me," but "that spoke in me"); or appear to men in sleep, and make communications through dreams, as we read in the Gospel, "Behold, the angel of the Lord appeared unto him in a dream, saying"? For these methods of communication seem to imply that the angels have not tangible bodies, and make it a very difficult question to solve how the patriarchs washed their feet, and how it was that Jacob wrestled with the angel in a way so unmistakably material. To ask questions like these, and to make such guesses as we can at the answers, is a useful exercise for the intellect, if the discussion be kept within proper bounds, and if we avoid the error of supposing ourselves to know what we do not know. For what is the necessity for affirming, or denying, or defining with accuracy on these subjects, and others like them, when we may without blame be entirely ignorant of them?

Chapter 60. —It is More Necessary to Be Able to Detect the Wiles of Satan When He Transforms Himself into an Angel of Light.

It is more necessary to use all our powers of discrimination and judgment when Satan transforms himself into an angel of light, lest by his wiles he should lead us astray into hurtful courses. For, while he only deceives the bodily senses, and does not pervert the mind from that true and sound judgment which enables a man to lead a life of faith, there is no danger to religion; or if, feigning himself to be good, he does or says the things that befit good angels, and we believe him to be good, the error is not one that is hurtful or dangerous to Christian faith. But when, through these means, which are alien to his nature, he goes on to lead us into courses of his own, then great watchfulness is necessary to detect, and refuse to follow, him. But how many men are fit to evade all his deadly wiles, unless God restrains and watches over them? The very difficulty of the matter, however, is useful in this respect, that it prevents men from trusting in themselves or in one another, and leads all to place their confidence in God alone. And certainly no pious man can doubt that this is most expedient for us.

Chapter 61. —The Church on Earth Has Been Redeemed from Sin by the Blood of a Mediator.

This part of the Church, then, which is made up of the holy angels and the hosts of God, shall become known to us in its true nature, when, at the end of the world, we shall be united with it in the common possession of everlasting happiness. But the other part, which, separated from it, wanders as a stranger on the earth, is better known to us, both because we belong to it, and because it is composed of men, and we too are men. This section of the Church has been redeemed from all sin by the blood of a Mediator who had no sin, and its song is: "If God be for us, who can be against us? He that spared not His own Son, but delivered Him up for us all." Now it was not for the angels that Christ died. Yet what was done for the redemption of man through His death was in a sense done for the angels, because the enmity which sin had put between men and the holy angels is removed, and friendship is restored between them, and by the redemption of man the gaps which the great apostasy left in the angelic host are filled up.

Chapter 62. —By the Sacrifice of Christ All Things are Restored, and Peace is Made Between Earth and Heaven.

And, of course, the holy angels, taught by God, in the eternal contemplation of whose truth their happiness consists, know how great a number of the human race are to supplement their ranks, and fill up the full tale of their citizenship. Wherefore the apostle says, that "all things are gathered together in one in Christ, both which are in heaven and which are on earth." The things which are in heaven are gathered together when what was lost therefrom in the fall of the angels is restored from among men; and the things which are on earth are gathered together, when those who are predestined to eternal life are redeemed from their old corruption. And thus, through that single sacrifice in which the Mediator was offered up, the one sacrifice of which the many victims under the law were types, heavenly things are brought into peace with earthly things, and earthly things with heavenly. Wherefore, as the same apostle says: "For it pleased the Father that in Him should all fullness dwell: and, having made peace through the blood of His cross, by Him to reconcile all things to Himself: by Him, I say, whether they be things in earth, or things in heaven."

Chapter 63. —The Peace of God, Which Reigned in Heaven, Passes All Understanding.

This peace, as Scripture saith, "passes all understanding," and cannot be known by us until we have come into the full possession of it. For in what sense are heavenly things reconciled, except they be reconciled to us, viz. by coming into harmony with us? For in heaven there is unbroken peace, both between all the intelligent creatures that exist there, and between these and their Creator. And this peace, as is said, passes all understanding; but this, of course, means our understanding, not that of those who always behold the face of their Father. We now, however great may be our human understanding, know but in part, and see through a glass darkly. But when we shall be equal unto the angels of God then we shall see face to face, as they do; and we shall have as great peace towards them as they have towards us, because we shall love them as much as we are loved by them. And so their peace shall be known to us: for our own peace shall be like to theirs, and as great as theirs, nor shall it then pass our understanding. But the peace of God, the peace which He cherishes towards us, shall undoubtedly pass not our understanding only, but theirs as well. And this must be so: for every rational creature which is happy derives its happiness from Him; He does not derive His from it. And in this view it is better to interpret "all" in the passage, "The peace of God passes all understanding," as admitting of no exception even in favor of the understanding of the holy angels: the only exception that can be made is that of God Himself. For, of course, His peace does not pass His own understanding.

Chapter 64. —Pardon of Sin Extends Over the Whole Mortal Life of the Saints, Which, Though Free from Crime, is Not Free from Sin.

But the angels even now are at peace with us when our sins are pardoned. Hence, in the order of the Creed, after the mention of the Holy Church is placed the remission of sins. For it is by this that the Church on earth stands: it is through this that what had been lost, and was found, is saved from being lost again. For, setting aside the grace of baptism, which is given as an antidote to original sin, so that what our birth imposes upon us, our new birth relieves us from (this grace, however, takes away all the actual sins also that have been committed in thought, word, and deed): setting aside, then, this great act of favor, whence commences man's restoration, and in which all our guilt, both original and actual, is washed away, the rest of our life from the time that we have the use of reason provides constant occasion for the remission of sins, however great may be our advance in righteousness. For the sons of God, as long as they live in this body of death, are in conflict with death. And although it is truly said of them, "As many as are led by the Spirit of God, they are the sons of God," yet they are led by the Spirit of God, and as the sons of God advance towards God under this drawback, that they are led also by their own spirit, weighted as it is by the corruptible body; and that, as the sons of men, under the influence of human affections, they fall back to their old level, and so sin. There is a difference, however. For although every crime is a sin, every sin is not a crime. And so we say that the life of holy men, as long as they remain in this mortal body, may be found without crime; but, as the Apostle John says, "If we say that we have no sin, we deceive ourselves, and the truth is not in us."

Chapter 65. —God Pardons Sins, But on Condition of Penitence, Certain Times for Which Have Been Fixed by the Law of the Church.

But even crimes themselves, however great, may be remitted in the Holy Church; and the mercy of God is never to be despaired of by men who truly repent, each according to the measure of his sin. And in the act of repentance, where a crime has been committed of such a nature as to cut off the sinner from the body of Christ, we are not to take account so much of the measure of time as of the measure of sorrow; for a broken and a contrite heart God doth not despise. But as the grief of one heart is frequently hid from another, and is not made known to others by words or other signs, when it is manifest to Him of whom it is said, "My groaning is not hid from Thee," those who govern the Church have rightly appointed times of penitence, that the Church in which the sins are remitted may be satisfied; and outside the Church sins are not remitted. For the Church alone has received the pledge of the Holy Spirit, without which there is no remission of sins—such, at least, as brings the pardoned to eternal life.

Chapter 66. —The Pardon of Sin Has Reference Chiefly to the Future Judgment.

Now the pardon of sin has reference chiefly to the future judgment. For, as far as this life is concerned, the saying of Scripture holds good: "A heavy yoke is upon the sons of Adam, from the day that they go out of their mother's womb, till the day that they return to the mother of all things." So that we see even infants, after baptism and regeneration, suffering from the infliction of divers evils: and thus we are given to understand, that all that is set forth in the sacraments of salvation refers rather to the hope of future good, than to the retaining or attaining of present blessings. For many sins seem in this world to be overlooked and visited with no punishment, whose punishment is reserved for the future (for it is not in vain that the day when Christ shall come as Judge of quick and dead is peculiarly named the day of judgment); just as, on the other hand, many sins are punished in this life, which nevertheless are pardoned, and shall bring down no punishment in the future life. Accordingly, about certain temporal punishments, which in this life are visited upon sinners, the apostle, addressing those whose sins are blotted out, and not reserved for the final judgment, says: "For if we would judge ourselves, we should not be judged. But when we are judged, we are chastened of the Lord, that we should not be condemned with the world."

Chapter 67. —Faith Without Works is Dead, and Cannot Save a Man.

It is believed, moreover, by some, that men who do not abandon the name of Christ, and who have been baptized in the Church by His baptism, and who have never been cut off from the Church by any schism or heresy, though they should live in the grossest sin and never either wash it away in penitence nor redeem it by almsgiving, but persevere in it persistently to the last day of their lives, shall be saved by fire; that is, that although they shall suffer a punishment by fire, lasting for a time proportionate to the magnitude of their crimes and misdeeds, they shall not be punished with everlasting fire. But those who believe this, and yet are Catholics, seem to me to be led astray by a kind of benevolent feeling natural to humanity. For Holy Scripture, when consulted, gives a very different answer. I have written a book on this subject, entitled Of Faith and Works, in which, to the best of my ability, God assisting me, I have shown from Scripture, that the faith which saves us is that which the Apostle Paul clearly enough describes when he says: "For in Jesus Christ neither circumcision availed anything, nor uncircumcision, but faith which worketh by love." But if it worketh evil, and not good, then without doubt, as the Apostle James says, "it is dead, being alone." The same apostle says again, "What doth it profit, my brethren, though a man say he hath faith, and have not works? Can faith save him?" And further, if a wicked man shall be saved by fire on account of his faith alone, and if this is what the blessed Apostle Paul means when he says, "But he himself shall be saved, yet so as by fire;" then faith without works can save a man, and what his fellow-apostle James says must be false. And that must be false which Paul himself says in another place: "Be not deceived: neither fornicators, nor idolaters, nor adulterers, nor effeminate, nor abusers of themselves with mankind, nor thieves, nor covetous, nor drunkards, nor revilers, nor extortioners; shall inherit the kingdom of God." For if those who persevere in these wicked courses shall nevertheless be saved because their faith in Christ, how can it be true that they shall not inherit the kingdom of God?

Chapter 68. —The True Sense of the Passage (I Cor. III. 11–15) About Those Who are Saved, Yet So as by Fire.

But as these most plain and unmistakable declarations of the apostles cannot be false, that obscure saying about those who build upon the foundation, Christ, not gold, silver, and precious stones, but wood, hay, and stubble (for it is these who, it is said, shall be saved, yet so as by fire, the merit of the foundation saving them), must be so interpreted as not to conflict with the plain statements quoted above. Now wood, hay, and stubble may, without incongruity, be understood to signify such an attachment to worldly things, however lawful these may be in themselves, that they cannot be lost without grief of mind. And though this grief burns, yet if Christ hold the place of foundation in the heart, —that is, if nothing be preferred to Him, and if the man, though burning with grief, is yet more willing to lose the things he loves so much than to lose Christ, —he is saved by fire. If, however, in time of temptation, he prefer to hold by temporal and earthly things rather than by Christ, he has not Christ as his foundation; for he puts earthly things in the first place, and in a building nothing comes before the foundation. Again, the fire of which the apostle speaks in this place must be such a fire as both men are made to pass through, that is, both the man who builds upon the foundation, gold, silver, precious stones, and the man who builds wood, hay, stubble. For he immediately adds: "The fire shall try every man's work, of what sort it is. If any man's work abide which he hath built thereupon, he shall receive a reward. If any man's work shall be burned, he shall suffer loss; but he himself shall be saved, yet so as by fire." The fire then shall prove, not the work of one of them only, but of both. Now the trial of adversity is a kind of fire which is plainly spoken of in another place: "The furnace proveth the potter's vessels: and the furnace of adversity just men." And this fire does in the course of this life act exactly in the way the apostle says. If it come into contact with two believers, one "caring for the things that belong to the Lord, how he may please the Lord," that is, building upon Christ the foundation, gold, silver, precious stones; the other "caring for the things that are of the world, how he may please his wife," that is, building upon the same foundation wood, hay, stubble,—the work of the former is not burned, because he has not given his love to things whose loss can cause him grief; but the work of the latter is burned, because things that are enjoyed with desire cannot be lost without pain. But since, by our supposition, even the latter prefers to lose these things rather than to lose Christ, and since he does not desert Christ out of fear of losing them, though he is grieved when he does lose them, he is saved, but it is so as by fire; because the grief for what he loved and has lost burns him. But it does not subvert nor consume him; for he is protected by his immoveable and incorruptible foundation.

Chapter 69. —It is Not Impossible that Some Believers May Pass Through a Purgatorial Fire in the Future Life.

And it is not impossible that something of the same kind may take place even after this life. It is a matter that may be inquired into, and either ascertained or left doubtful, whether some believers shall pass through a kind of purgatorial fire, and in proportion as they have loved with more or less devotion the goods that perish, be less or more quickly delivered from it. This cannot, however, be the case of any of those of whom it is said, that they "shall not inherit the kingdom of God," unless after suitable repentance their sins be forgiven them. When I say "suitable," I mean that they are not to be unfruitful in almsgiving; for Holy Scripture lays so much stress on this virtue, that our Lord tells us beforehand, that He will ascribe no merit to those on His right hand but that they abound in it, and no defect to those on His left hand but their want of it, when He shall say to the former, "Come, ye blessed of my Father, inherit the kingdom," and to the latter, "Depart from me, ye cursed, into everlasting fire."

Chapter 70. —Almsgiving Will Not Atone for Sin Unless the Life Be Changed.

We must beware, however, lest anyone should suppose that gross sins, such as are committed by those who shall not inherit the kingdom of God, may be daily perpetrated, and daily atoned for by almsgiving. The life must be changed for the better; and almsgiving must be used to propitiate God for past sins, not to purchase impunity for the commission of such sins in the future. For He has given no man license to sin, although in His mercy He may blot out sins that are already committed, if we do not neglect to make proper satisfaction.

Chapter 71. —The Daily Prayer of the Believer Makes Satisfaction for the Trivial Sins that Daily Stain His Life.

Now the daily prayer of the believer makes satisfaction for those daily sins of a momentary and trivial kind which are necessary incidents of this life. For he can say, "Our Father which art in heaven," seeing that to such a Father he is now born again of water and of the Spirit. And this prayer certainly takes away the very small sins of daily life. It takes away also those which at one time made the life of the believer very wicked, but which, now that he is changed for the better by repentance, he has given up, provided that as truly as he says, "Forgive us our debts" (for there is no want of debts to be forgiven), so truly does he say, "as we forgive our debtors;" that is, provided he does what he says he does: for to forgive a man who asks for pardon, is really to give alms.

Chapter 72. —There are Many Kinds of Alms, the Giving of Which Assists to Procure Pardon for Our Sins.

And on this principle of interpretation, our Lord's saying, "Give alms of such things as ye have, and, behold, all things are clean unto you," applies to every useful act that a man does in mercy. Not only, then, the man who gives food to the hungry, drink to the thirsty, clothing to the naked, hospitality to the stranger, shelter to the fugitive, who visits the sick and the imprisoned, ransoms the captive, assists the weak, leads the blind, comforts the sorrowful, heals the sick, puts the wanderer on the right path, gives advice to the perplexed, and supplies the wants of the needy,—not this man only, but the man who pardons the sinner also gives alms; and the man who corrects with blows, or restrains by any kind of discipline one over whom he has power, and who at the same time forgives from the heart the sin by which he was injured, or prays that it may be forgiven, is also a giver of alms, not only in that he forgives, or prays for forgiveness for the sin, but also in that he rebukes and corrects the sinner: for in this, too, he shows mercy. Now much good is bestowed upon unwilling recipients, when their advantage and not their pleasure is consulted; and they themselves frequently prove to be their own enemies, while their true friends are those whom they take for their enemies, and to whom in their blindness they return evil for good. (A Christian, indeed, is not permitted to return evil even for evil.) And thus, there are many kinds of alms, by giving of which we assist to procure the pardon of our sins.

Chapter 73. —The Greatest of All Alms is to Forgive Our Debtors and to Love Our Enemies.

But none of those is greater than to forgive from the heart a sin that has been committed against us. For it is a comparatively small thing to wish well to, or even to do good to, a man who has done no evil to you. It is a much higher thing, and is the result of the most exalted goodness, to love your enemy, and always to wish well to, and when you have the opportunity, to do good to, the man who wishes you ill, and, when he can, does you harm. This is to obey the command of God: "Love your enemies, do good to them that hate you, and pray for them which persecute you." But seeing that this is a frame of mind only reached by the perfect sons of God, and that though every believer ought to strive after it, and by prayer to God and earnest struggling with himself endeavor to bring his soul up to this standard, yet a degree of goodness so high can hardly belong to so great a multitude as we believe are heard when they use this petition, "Forgive us our debts, as we forgive our debtors;" in view of all this, it cannot be doubted that the implied undertaking is fulfilled if a man, though he has not yet attained to loving his enemy, yet, when asked by one who has sinned against him to forgive him his sin, does forgive him from his heart. For he certainly desires to be himself forgiven when he prays, "as we forgive our debtors," that is, Forgive us our debts when we beg forgiveness, as we forgive our debtors when they beg forgiveness from us.

Chapter 74. —God Does Not Pardon the Sins of Those Who Do Not from the Heart Forgive Others.

Now, he who asks forgiveness of the man against whom he has sinned, being moved by his sin to ask forgiveness, cannot be counted an enemy in such a sense that it should be as difficult to love him now as it was when he was engaged in active hostility. And the man who does not from his heart forgive him who repents of his sin, and asks forgiveness, need not suppose that his own sins are forgiven of God. For the Truth cannot lie. And what reader or hearer of the Gospel can have failed to notice, that the same person who said, "I am the Truth," taught us also this form of prayer; and in order to impress this particular petition deeply upon our minds, said, "For if ye forgive men their trespasses, your heavenly Father will also forgive you; but if ye forgive not men their trespasses, neither will your Father forgive your trespasses"? The man whom the thunder of this warning does not awaken is not asleep, but dead; and yet so powerful is that voice, that it can awaken even the dead.

Chapter 75. —The Wicked and the Unbelieving are Not Made Clean by the Giving of Alms, Except They Be Born Again.

Assuredly, then, those who live in gross wickedness, and take no care to reform their lives and manners, and yet amid all their crimes and vices do not cease to give frequent alms, in vain take comfort to themselves from the saying of our Lord: "Give alms of such things as ye have; and, behold, all things are clean unto you." For they do not understand how far this saying reaches. But that they may understand this, let them hear what He says. For we read in the Gospel as follows: "And as He spoke, a certain Pharisee besought Him to dine with him; and He went in, and sat down to meat. And when the Pharisee saw it, he marveled that He had not first washed before dinner. And the Lord said unto him, Now do ye Pharisees make clean the outside of the cup and the platter; but your inward part is full of ravening and wickedness. Ye fools, did not he that made that which is without, make that which is within also? But rather give alms of such things as ye have; and, behold, all things are clean unto you." Are we to understand this as meaning that to the Pharisees who have not the faith of Christ all things are clean, if only they give alms in the way these men count almsgiving, even though they have never believed in Christ, nor been born again of water and of the Spirit? But the fact is, that all are unclean who are not made clean by the faith of Christ, according to the expression, "purifying their hearts by faith;" and that the apostle says, "Unto them that are defiled and unbelieving is nothing pure; but even their mind and conscience is defiled." How, then, could all things be clean to the Pharisees, even though they gave alms, if they were not believers? And how could they be believers if they were not willing to have faith in Christ, and to be born again of His grace? And yet what they heard is true: "Give alms of such things as ye have; and, behold, all things are clean unto you."

Chapter 76. —To Give Alms Aright, We Should Begin with Ourselves, and Have Pity Upon Our Own Souls.

For the man who wishes to give aims as he ought, should begin with himself, and give to himself first. For almsgiving is a work of mercy; and most truly is it said, "To have mercy on thy soul is pleasing to God." And for this end are we born again, that we should be pleasing to God, who is justly displeased with that which we brought with us when we were born. This is our first alms, which we give to ourselves when, through the mercy of a pitying God, we find that we are ourselves wretched, and confess the justice of His judgment by which we are made wretched, of which the apostle says, "The judgment was by one to condemnation;" and praise the greatness of His love, of which the same preacher of grace says, "God commendeth His love toward us, in that, while we were yet sinners, Christ died for us:" and thus judging truly of our own misery, and loving God with the love which He has Himself bestowed, we lead a holy and virtuous life. But the Pharisees, while they gave as alms the tithe of all their fruits, even the most insignificant, passed over judgment and the love of God, and so did not commence their alms-giving at home, and extend their pity to themselves in the first instance. And it is about this order of love that it is said, "Love thy neighbor as thyself." When, then, our Lord had rebuked them because they made themselves clean on the outside, but within were full of ravening and wickedness, He advised them, in the exercise of that charity which each man owes to himself in the first instance, to make clean the inward parts. "But rather," He says, "give alms of such things as ye have; and, behold, all things are clean unto you." Then, to show what it was that He advised, and what they took no pains to do, and to show that He did not overlook or forget their almsgiving, "But woe unto you, Pharisees!" He says; as if He meant to say: I indeed advise you to give alms which shall make all things clean unto you; "but woe unto you! for ye tithe mint, and rue, and all manner of herbs;" as if He meant to say: I know these alms of yours, and ye need not think that I am now admonishing you in respect of such things; "and pass over judgment and the love of God," an alms by which ye might have been made clean from all inward impurity, so that even the bodies which ye are now washing would have been clean to you. For this is the import of "all things," both inward and outward things, as we read in another place: "Cleanse first that which is within, that the outside may be clean also." But lest He might appear to despise the alms which they were giving out of the fruits of the earth, He says: "These ought ye to have done," referring to judgment and the love of God, "and not to leave the other undone," referring to the giving of the tithes.

Chapter 77. —If We Would Give Alms to Ourselves, We Must Flee Iniquity; For He Who Loveth Iniquity Hated His Soul.

Those, then, who think that they can by giving alms, however profuse, whether in money or in kind, purchase for themselves the privilege of persisting with impunity in their monstrous crimes and hideous vices, need not thus deceive themselves. For not only do they commit these sins, but they love them so much that they would like to go on forever committing them, if only they could do so with impunity. Now, he who loveth iniquity hated his own soul; and he who hated his own soul is not merciful but cruel towards it. For in loving it according to the world, he hated it according to God. But if he desired to give alms to it which should make all things clean unto him, he would hate it according to the world, and love it according to God. Now no one gives alms unless he receive what he gives from one who is not in want of it. Therefore it is said, "His mercy shall meet me."

Chapter 78. —What Sins are Trivial and What Heinous is a Matter for God's Judgment.

Now, what sins are trivial and what heinous is not a matter to be decided by man's judgment, but by the judgment of God. For it is plain that the apostles themselves have given an indulgence in the case of certain sins: take, for example, what the Apostle Paul says to those who are married: "Defraud ye not one the other, except it be with consent for a time, that ye may give yourselves to fasting and prayer: and come together again, that Satan tempt you not for your incontinency." Now it is possible that it might not have been considered a sin to have intercourse with a spouse, not with a view to the procreation of children, which is the great blessing of marriage, but for the sake of carnal pleasure, and to save the incontinent from being led by their weakness into the deadly sin of fornication, or adultery, or another form of uncleanness which it is shameful even to name, and into which it is possible that they might be drawn by lust under the temptation of Satan. It is possible, I say, that this might not have been considered a sin, had the apostle not added: "But I speak this by permission, and not of commandment." Who, then, can deny that it is a sin, when confessedly it is only by apostolic authority that permission is granted to those who do it? Another case of the same kind is where he says: "Dare any of you, having a matter against another, go to law before the unjust, and not before the saints?" And shortly afterwards: "If then ye have judgments of things pertaining to this life, set them to judge who are least esteemed in the Church. I speak to your shame. Is it so, that there is not a wise man among you? no, not one that shall be able to judge between his brethren? But brother goeth to law with brother, and that before the unbelievers." Now it might have been supposed in this case that it is not a sin to have a quarrel with another, that the only sin is in wishing to have it adjudicated upon outside the Church, had not the apostle immediately added: "Now therefore there is utterly a fault among you, because ye go to law with one another." And lest anyone should excuse himself by saying that he had a just cause, and was suffering wrong, and that he only wished the sentence of the judges to remove his wrong, the apostle immediately anticipates such thoughts and excuses, and says: "Why do ye not rather take wrong? Why do ye not rather suffer yourselves to be defrauded?" Thus bringing us back to our Lord's saying, "If any man will sue thee at the law, and take away thy coat, let him have thy cloak also;" and again, "Of him that taketh away thy goods, ask them not again." Therefore, our Lord has forbidden His followers to go to law with other men about worldly affairs. And carrying out this principle, the apostle here declares that to do so is "altogether a fault." But when, notwithstanding, he grants his permission to have such cases between brethren decided in the Church, other brethren adjudicating, and only sternly forbids them to be carried outside the Church, it is manifest that here again an indulgence is extended to the infirmities of the weak. It is in view, then, of these sins, and others of the same sort, and of others again more trifling still, which consist of offenses in words and thought (as the Apostle James confesses, "In many things we offend all"), that we need to pray every day and often to the Lord, saying, "Forgive us our debts," and to add in truth and sincerity, "as we forgive our debtors."

Chapter 79. —Sins Which Appear Very Trifling, are Sometimes in Reality Very Serious.

Again, there are some sins which would be considered very trifling, if the Scriptures did not show that they are really very serious. For who would suppose that the man who says to his brother, "Thou fool," is in danger of hell-fire, did not He who is the Truth say so? To the wound, however, He immediately applies the cure, giving a rule for reconciliation with one's offended brother: "Therefore, if thou bring thy gift to the altar, and there remembers that thy brother hath ought against thee; leave there thy gift before the altar, and go thy way: first be reconciled to thy brother, and then come and offer thy gift." Again, who would suppose that it was so great a sin to observe days, and months, and times, and years, as those do who are anxious or unwilling to begin anything on certain days, or in certain months or years, because the vain doctrines of men lead them to think such times lucky or unlucky, had we not the means of estimating the greatness of the evil from the fear expressed by the apostle, who says to such men, "I am afraid of you, lest I have bestowed upon you labor in vain"?

Chapter 80. —Sins, However Great and Detestable, Seem Trivial When We are Accustomed to Them.

Add to this, that sins, however great and detestable they may be, are looked upon as trivial, or as not sins at all, when men get accustomed to them; and so far does this go, that such sins are not only not concealed, but are boasted of, and published far and wide; and thus, as it is written, "The wicked boasted of his heart's desire, and blessed the covetous, whom the Lord abhorred." Iniquity of this kind is in Scripture called a cry. You have an instance in the prophet Isaiah, in the case of the evil vineyard: "He looked for judgment, but behold oppression; for righteousness, but behold a cry." Whence also the expression in Genesis: "The cry of Sodom and Gomorrah is great," because in these cities crimes were not only not punished, but were openly committed, as if under the protection of the law. And so in our own times: many forms of sin, though not just the same as those of Sodom and Gomorrah, are now so openly and habitually practiced, that not only dare we not excommunicate a layman, we dare not even degrade a clergyman, for the commission of them. So that when, a few years ago, I was expounding the Epistle to the Galatians, in commenting on that very place where the apostle says, "I am afraid of you, lest I have bestowed labor upon you in vain," I was compelled to exclaim, "Woe to the sins of men! for it is only when we are not accustomed to them that we shrink from them: when once we are accustomed to them, though the blood of the Son of God was poured out to wash them away, though they are so great that the kingdom of God is wholly shut against them, constant familiarity leads to the toleration of them all, and habitual toleration leads to the practice of many of them. And grant, O Lord, that we may not come to practice all that we have not the power to hinder." But I shall see whether the extravagance of grief did not betray me into rashness of speech.

Chapter 81. —There are Two Causes of Sin, Ignorance and Weakness; And We Need Divine Help to Overcome Both.

I shall now say this, which I have often said before in other places of my works. There are two causes that lead to sin: either we do not yet know our duty, or we do not perform the duty that we know. The former is the sin of ignorance, the latter of weakness. Now against these it is our duty to struggle; but we shall certainly be beaten in the fight, unless we are helped by God, not only to see our duty, but also, when we clearly see it, to make the love of righteousness stronger in us than the love of earthly things, the eager longing after which, or the fear of losing which, leads us with our eyes open into known sin. In the latter case we are not only sinners, for we are so even when we err through ignorance, but we are also transgressors of the law; for we leave undone what we know we ought to do, and we do what we know we ought not to do. Wherefore not only ought we to pray for pardon when we have sinned, saying, "Forgive us our debts, as we forgive our debtors;" but we ought to pray for guidance, that we may be kept from sinning, saying, "and lead us not into temptation." And we are to pray to Him of whom the Psalmist says, "The Lord is my light and my salvation:" my light, for He removes my ignorance; my salvation, for He takes away my infirmity.

Chapter 82. —The Mercy of God is Necessary to True Repentance.

Now even penance itself, when by the law of the Church there is sufficient reason for its being gone through, is frequently evaded through infirmity; for shame is the fear of losing pleasure when the good opinion of men gives more pleasure than the righteousness which leads a man to humble himself in penitence. Wherefore the mercy of God is necessary not only when a man repents, but even to lead him to repent. How else explain what the apostle says of certain persons: "if God peradventure will give them repentance"? And before Peter wept bitterly, we are told by the evangelist, "The Lord turned, and looked upon him."

Chapter 83. —The Man Who Despises the Mercy of God is Guilty of the Sin Against the Holy Ghost.

Now the man who, not believing that sins are remitted in the Church, despises this great gift of God's mercy, and persists to the last day of his life in his obstinacy of heart, is guilty of the unpardonable sin against the Holy Ghost, in whom Christ forgives sins. But this difficult question I have discussed as clearly as I could in a book devoted exclusively to this one point.

Chapter 84. —The Resurrection of the Body Gives Rise to Numerous Questions.

Now, as to the resurrection of the body, —not a resurrection such as some have had, who came back to life for a time and died again, but a resurrection to eternal life, as the body of Christ Himself rose again, —I do not see how I can discuss the matter briefly, and at the same time give a satisfactory answer to all the questions that are ordinarily raised about it. Yet that the bodies of all men—both those who have been born and those who shall be born, both those who have died and those who shall die—shall be raised again, no Christian ought to have the shadow of a doubt.

Chapter 85. —The Case of Abortive Conceptions.

Hence in the first place arises a question about abortive conceptions, which have indeed been born in the mother's womb, but not so born that they could be born again. For if we shall decide that these are to rise again, we cannot object to any conclusion that may be drawn regarding those which are fully formed. Now who is there that is not rather disposed to think that unformed abortions perish, like seeds that have never fructified? But who will dare to deny, though he may not dare to affirm, that at the resurrection every defect in the form shall be supplied, and that thus the perfection which time would have brought shall not be wanting, any more than the blemishes which time did bring shall be present: so that the nature shall neither want anything suitable and in harmony with it that length of days would have added, nor be debased by the presence of anything of an opposite kind that length of days has added; but that what is not yet complete shall be completed, just as what has been injured shall be renewed.

Chapter 86. —If They Have Ever Lived, They Must of Course Have Died, and Therefore Shall Have a Share in the Resurrection of the Dead.

And therefore, the following question may be very carefully inquired into and discussed by learned men, though I do not know whether it is in man's power to resolve it: At what time the infant begins to live in the womb: whether life exists in a latent form before it manifests itself in the motions of the living being. To deny that the young who are cut out limb by limb from the womb, lest if they were left there dead the mother should die too, have never been alive, seems too audacious. Now, from the time that a man begins to live, from that time it is possible for him to die. And if he die, wheresoever death may overtake him, I cannot discover on what principle he can be denied an interest in the resurrection of the dead.

Chapter 87. —The Case of Monstrous Births.

We are not justified in affirming even of monstrosities, which are born and live, however quickly they may die, that they shall not rise again, nor that they shall rise again in their deformity, and not rather with an amended and perfected body. God forbid that the double limbed man who was lately born in the East, of whom an account was brought by most trustworthy brethren who had seen him, —an account which the presbyter Jerome, of blessed memory, left in writing; —God forbid, I say, that we should think that at the resurrection there shall be one man with double limbs, and not two distinct men, as would have been the case had twins been born. And so other births, which, because they have either a superfluity or a defect, or because they are very much deformed, are called monstrosities, shall at the resurrection be restored to the normal shape of man; and so each single soul shall possess its own body; and no bodies shall cohere together even though they were born in cohesion, but each separately shall possess all the members which constitute a complete human body.

Chapter 88. —The Material of the Body Never Perishes.

Nor does the earthly material out of which men's mortal bodies are created ever perish; but though it may crumble into dust and ashes, or be dissolved into vapors and exhalations, though it may be transformed into the substance of other bodies, or dispersed into the elements, though it should become food for beasts or men, and be changed into their flesh, it returns in a moment of time to that human soul which animated it at the first, and which caused it to become man, and to live and grow.

Chapter 89. —But This Material May Be Differently Arranged in the Resurrection Body.

And this earthly material, which when the soul leaves it becomes a corpse, shall not at the resurrection be so restored as that the parts into which it is separated, and which under various forms and appearances become parts of other things (though they shall all return to the same body from which they were separated), must necessarily return to the same parts of the body in which they were originally situated. For otherwise, to suppose that the hair recovers all that our frequent clippings and shavings have taken away from it, and the nails all that we have so often pared off, presents to the imagination such a picture of ugliness and deformity, as to make the resurrection of the body all but incredible. But just as if a statue of some soluble metal were either melted by fire, or broken into dust, or reduced to a shapeless mass, and a sculptor wished to restore it from the same quantity of metal, it would make no difference to the completeness of the work what part of the statue any given particle of the material was put into, as long as the restored statue contained all the material of the original one; so God, the Artificer of marvelous and unspeakable power, shall with marvelous and unspeakable rapidity restore our body, using up the whole material of which it originally consisted. Nor will it affect the completeness of its restoration whether hairs return to hairs, and nails to nails, or whether the part of these that had perished be changed into flesh, and called to take its place in another part of the body, the great Artist taking careful heed that nothing shall be unbecoming or out of place.

Chapter 90. —If There Be Differences and Inequalities Among the Bodies of Those Who Rise Again, There Shall Be Nothing Offensive or Disproportionate in Any.

Nor does it necessarily follow that there shall be differences of stature among those who rise again, because they were of different statures during life; nor is it certain that the lean shall rise again in their former leanness, and the fat in their former fatness. But if it is part of the Creator's design that each should preserve his own peculiarities of feature, and retain a recognizable likeness to his former self, while regarding other bodily advantages all should be equal, then the material of which each is composed may be so modified that none of it shall be lost, and that any defect may be supplied by Him who can create at His will out of nothing. But if in the bodies of those who rise again there shall be a well-ordered inequality, such as there is in the voices that make up a full harmony, then the material of each man's body shall be so dealt with that it shall form a man fit for the assemblies of the angels, and one who shall bring nothing among them to jar upon their sensibilities. And assuredly nothing that is unseemly shall be there; but whatever shall be there shall be graceful and becoming: for if anything is not seemly, neither shall it be.

Chapter 91. —The Bodies of the Saints Shall at The Resurrection Be Spiritual Bodies.

The bodies of the saints, then, shall rise again free

from every defect, from every blemish, as from all corruption, weight, and impediment. For their ease of movement shall be as complete as their happiness. Whence their bodies have been called spiritual, though undoubtedly they shall be bodies and not spirits. For just as now the body is called animate, though it is a body, and not a soul [anima], so then the body shall be called spiritual, though it shall be a body, not a spirit. Hence, as far as regards the corruption which now weighs down the soul, and the vices which urge the flesh to lust against the spirit, it shall not then be flesh, but body; for there are bodies which are called celestial. Wherefore it is said, "Flesh and blood cannot inherit the kingdom of God;" and, as if in explanation of this, "neither doth corruption inherit incorruption." What the apostle first called "flesh and blood," he afterwards calls "corruption;" and what he first called "the kingdom of God," he afterwards calls "incorruption." But as far as regards the substance, even then it shall be flesh. For even after the resurrection the body of Christ was called flesh. The apostle, however, says: "It is sown a natural body; it is raised a spiritual body;" because so perfect shah then be the harmony between flesh and spirit, the spirit keeping alive the subjugated flesh without the need of any nourishment, that no part of our nature shall be in discord with another; but as we shall be free from enemies without, so we shall not have ourselves for enemies within.

Chapter 92. —The Resurrection of the Lost.

But as for those who, out of the mass of perdition caused by the first man's sin, are not redeemed through the one Mediator between God and man, they too shall rise again, each with his own body, but only to be punished with the devil and his angels. Now, whether they shall rise again with all their diseases and deformities of body, bringing with them the diseased and deformed limbs which they possessed here, it would be labor lost to inquire. For we need not weary ourselves speculating about their health or their beauty, which are matters uncertain, when their eternal damnation is a matter of certainty. Nor need we inquire in what sense their body shall be incorruptible, if it be susceptible of pain; or in what sense corruptible, if it be free from the possibility of death. For there is no true life except where there is happiness in life, and no true incorruption except where health is unbroken by any pain. When, however, the unhappy are not permitted to die, then, if I may so speak, death itself dies not; and where pain without intermission afflicts the soul, and never comes to an end, corruption itself is not completed. This is called in Holy Scripture "the second death."

Chapter 93. —Both the First and the Second Deaths are the Consequence of Sin. Punishment is Proportioned to Guilt.

And neither the first death, which takes place when the soul is compelled to leave the body, nor the second death, which takes place when the soul is not permitted to leave the suffering body, would have been inflicted on man had no one sinned. And, of course, the mildest punishment of all will fall upon those who have added no actual sin, to the original sin they brought with them; and as for the rest who have added such actual sins, the punishment of each will be the more tolerable in the next world, according as his iniquity has been less in this world.

Chapter 94. —The Saints Shall Know More Fully in the Next World the Benefits They Have Received by Grace.

Thus, when reprobate angels and men are left to endure everlasting punishment, the saints shall know more fully the benefits they have received by grace. Then, in contemplation of the actual facts, they shall see more clearly the meaning of the expression in the psalms, "I will sing of mercy and judgment;" for it is only of unmerited mercy that any is redeemed, and only in well-merited judgment that any is condemned.

Chapter 95. —God's Judgments Shall Then Be Explained.

Then shall be made clear much that is now dark. For example, when of two infants, whose cases seem in all respects alike, one by the mercy of God chosen to Himself, and the other is by His justice abandoned (wherein the one who is chosen may recognize what was of justice due to himself, had not mercy intervened); why, of these two, the one should have been chosen rather than the other, is to us an insoluble problem. And again, why miracles were not wrought in the presence of men who would have repented at the working of the miracles, while they were wrought in the presence of others who, it was known, would not repent. For our Lord says most distinctly: "Woe unto thee, Chorazin! woe unto thee, Bethsaida! for if the mighty works, which were done in you, had been done in Tyre and Sidon, they would have repented long ago in sackcloth and ashes." And assuredly there was no injustice in God's not willing that they should be saved, though they could have been saved had He so willed it. Then shall be seen in the clearest light of wisdom what with the pious is now a faith, though it is not yet a matter of certain knowledge, how sure, how unchangeable, and how effectual is the will of God; how many things He can do which He does not will to do, though willing nothing which He cannot perform; and how true is the song of the psalmist, "But our God is in the heavens; He hath done whatsoever He hath pleased." And this certainly is not true, if God has ever willed anything that He has not performed; and, still worse, if it was the will of man that hindered the Omnipotent from doing what He pleased. Nothing, therefore, happens but by the will of the Omnipotent, He either permitting it to be done, or Himself doing it.

Chapter 96. —The Omnipotent God Does Well Even in the Permission of Evil.

Nor can we doubt that God does well even in the permission of what is evil. For He permits it only in the justice of His judgment. And surely all that is just is good. Although, therefore, evil, in so far as it is evil, is not a good; yet the fact that evil as well as good exists, is a good. For if it were not a good that evil should exist, its existence would not be permitted by the omnipotent Good, who without doubt can as easily refuse to permit what He does not wish, as bring about what He does wish. And if we do not believe this, the very first sentence of our creed is endangered, wherein we profess to believe in God the Father Almighty. For He is not truly called Almighty if He cannot do whatsoever He pleases, or if the power of His almighty will is hindered by the will of any creature whatsoever.

Chapter 97. —In What Sense Does the Apostle Say that "God Will Have All Men to Be Saved," When, as a Matter of Fact, All are Not Saved?

Hence, we must inquire in what sense is said of God what the apostle has mostly truly said: "Who will have all men to be saved." For, as a matter of fact, not all, nor even a majority, are saved: so that it would seem that what God wills is not done, man's will interfering with, and hindering the will of God. When we ask the reason why all men are not saved, the ordinary answer is: "Because men themselves are not willing." This, indeed cannot be said of infants, for it is not in their power either to will or not to will. But if we could attribute to their will the childish movements they make at baptism, when they make all the resistance they can, we should say that even they are not willing to be saved. Our Lord says plainly, however, in the Gospel, when upbraiding the impious city: "How often would I have gathered thy children together, even as a hen gathered her chickens under her wings, and ye would not!" as if the will of God had been overcome by the will of men, and when the weakest stood in the way with their want of will, the will of the strongest could not be carried out. And where is that omnipotence which hath done all that it pleased on earth and in heaven, if God willed to gather together the children of Jerusalem, and did not accomplish it? or rather, Jerusalem was not willing that her children should be gathered together? But even though she was unwilling, He gathered together as many of her children as He wished: for He does not will some things and do them, and will others and do them not; but "He hath done all that He pleased in heaven and in earth."

Chapter 98. —Predestination to Eternal Life is Wholly of God's Free Grace.

And, moreover, who will be so foolish and blasphemous as to say that God cannot change the evil wills of men, whichever, whenever, and wheresoever He chooses, and direct them to what is good? But when He does this He does it of mercy; when He does it not, it is of justice that He does it not for "He hath mercy on whom He will have mercy, and whom He will He hardeneth." And when the apostle said this, he was illustrating the grace of God, in connection with which he had just spoken of the twins in the womb of Rebecca, "who being not yet born, neither having done any good or evil that the purpose of God according to election might stand, not of works, but of Him that calleth, it was said unto her, The elder shall serve the younger." And in reference to this matter he quotes another prophetic testimony: "Jacob have I loved, but Esau have I hated." But perceiving how what he had said might affect those who could not penetrate by their understanding the depth of this grace: "What shall we say then?" he says: "Is there unrighteousness with God? God forbid." For it seems unjust that, in the absence of any merit or demerit, from good or evil works, God should love the one and hate the other. Now, if the apostle had wished us to understand that there were future good works of the one, and evil works of the other, which of course God foreknew, he would never have said, "not of works," but, "of future works," and in that way would have solved the difficulty, or rather there would then have been no difficulty to solve. As it is, however, after answering, "God forbid;" that is, God forbid that there should be unrighteousness with God; he goes on to prove that there is no unrighteousness in God's doing this, and says: "For He saith to Moses, I will have mercy on whom I will have mercy, and I will have compassion on whom I will have compassion." Now, who but a fool would think that God was unrighteous, either in inflicting penal justice on those who had earned it, or in extending mercy to the unworthy? Then he draws his conclusion: "So then it is not of him that willeth, nor of him that runneth, but of God that showed mercy." Thus both the twins were born children of wrath, not on account of any works of their own, but because they were bound in the fetters of that original condemnation which came through Adam. But He who said, "I will have mercy on whom I will have mercy," loved Jacob of His undeserved grace, and hated Esau of His deserved judgment. And as this judgment was due to both, the former learnt from the case of the latter that the fact of the same punishment not falling upon himself gave him no room to glory in any merit of his own, but only in the riches of the divine grace; because "it is not of him that willeth, nor of him that runneth, but of God that showed mercy." And indeed the whole face, and, if I may use the expression, every lineament of the countenance of Scripture conveys by a very profound analogy this wholesome warning to everyone who looks carefully into it, that he who glories should glory in the Lord.

Chapter 99. —As God's Mercy is Free, So His Judgments are Just, and Cannot Be Gainsaid.

Now after commending the mercy of God, saying, "So it is not of him that willeth, nor of him that runneth, but of God that showed mercy," that he might commend His justice also (for the man who does not obtain mercy finds, not iniquity, but justice, there being no iniquity with God), he immediately adds: "For the scripture saith unto Pharoah, Even for this same purpose have I raised thee up, that I might show my power in thee, and that my name might be declared throughout all the earth." And then he draws a conclusion that applies to both, that is, both to His mercy and His justice: "Therefore hath He mercy on whom He will have mercy, and whom He will He hardeneth." "He hath mercy" of His great goodness, "He hardeneth" without any injustice; so that neither can he that is pardoned glory in any merit of his own, nor he that is condemned complain of anything but his own demerit. For it is grace alone that separates the redeemed from the lost, all having been involved in one common perdition through their common origin. Now if anyone, on hearing this, should say, "Why doth He yet find fault? for who hath resisted His will?" as if a man ought not to be blamed for being bad, because God hath mercy on whom He will have mercy, and whom He will He hardeneth, God forbid that we should be ashamed to answer as we see the apostle answered: "Nay, but, O man, who art thou that replies against God? Shall the thing formed say to Him that formed it, Why hast Thou made me thus? Hath not the potter power over the clay, of the same lump to make one vessel unto honor, and another unto dishonor?" Now some foolish people, think that in this place the apostle had no answer to give; and for want of a reason to render, rebuked the presumption of his interrogator. But there is great weight in this saying: "Nay, but, O man, who art thou?" and in such a matter as this it suggests to a man in a single word the limits of his capacity, and at the same time does in reality convey an important reason. For if a man does not understand these matters, who is he that he should reply against God? And if he does understand them, he finds no further room for reply. For then he perceives that the whole human race was condemned in its rebellious head by a divine judgment so just, that if not a single member of the race had been redeemed, no one could justly have questioned the justice of God; and that it was right that those who are redeemed should be redeemed in such a way as to show, by the greater number who are unredeemed and left in their just condemnation, what the whole race deserved, and whither the deserved judgment of God would lead even the redeemed, did not His undeserved mercy interpose, so that every mouth might be stopped of those who wish to glory in their own merits, and that he that glories might glory in the Lord.

Chapter 100. —The Will of God is Never Defeated, Though Much is Done that is Contrary to His Will.

These are the great works of the Lord, sought out according to all His pleasure, and so wisely sought out, that when the intelligent creation, both angelic and human, sinned, doing not His will but their own, He used the very will of the creature which was working in opposition to the Creator's will as an instrument for carrying out His will, the supremely Good thus turning to good account even what is evil, to the condemnation of those whom in His justice He has predestined to punishment, and to the salvation of those whom in His mercy He has predestined to grace. For, as far as relates to their own consciousness, these creatures did what God wished not to be done: but in view of God's omnipotence, they could in no wise effect their purpose. For in the very fact that they acted in opposition to His will, His will concerning them was fulfilled. And hence it is that "the works of the Lord are great, sought out according to all His pleasure," because in a way unspeakably strange and wonderful, even what is done in opposition to His will does not defeat His will. For it would not be done did He not permit it (and of course His permission is not unwilling, but willing); nor would a Good Being permit evil to be done only that in His omnipotence He can turn evil into good.

Chapter 101. —The Will of God, which is Always Good, is Sometimes Fulfilled Through the Evil Will of Man.

Sometimes, however, a man in the goodness of his will desires something that God does not desire, even though God's will is also good, nay, much more fully and more surely good (for His will never can be evil): for example, if a good son is anxious that his father should live, when it is God's good will that he should die. Again, it is possible for a man with evil will to desire what God wills in His goodness: for example, if a bad son wishes his father to die, when this is also the will of God. It is plain that the former wishes what God does not wish, and that the latter wishes what God does wish; and yet the filial love of the former is more in harmony with the good will of God, though its desire is different from God's, than the want of filial affection of the latter, though its desire is the same as God's. So necessary is it, in determining whether a man's desire is one to be approved or disapproved, to consider what it is proper for man, and what it is proper for God, to desire, and what is in each case the real motive of the will. For God accomplishes some of His purposes, which of course are all good, through the evil desires of wicked men: for example, it was through the wicked designs of the Jews, working out the good purpose of the Father, that Christ was slain and this event was so truly good, that when the Apostle Peter expressed his unwillingness that it should take place, he was designated Satan by Him who had come to be slain. How good seemed the intentions of the pious believers who were unwilling that Paul should go up to Jerusalem lest the evils which Agabus had foretold should there befall him! And yet it was God's purpose that he should suffer these evils for preaching the faith of Christ, and thereby become a witness for Christ. And this purpose of His, which was good, God did not fulfill through the good counsels of the Christians, but through the evil counsels of the Jews; so that those who opposed His purpose were more truly His servants than those who were the willing instruments of its accomplishment.

Chapter 102. —The Will of the Omnipotent God is Never Defeated, and is Never Evil.

But however strong may be the purposes either of angels or of men, whether of good or bad, whether these purposes fall in with the will of God or run counter to it, the will of the Omnipotent is never defeated; and His will never can be evil; because even when it inflicts evil it is just, and what is just is certainly not evil. The omnipotent God, then, whether in mercy He pities whom He will, or in judgment hardeneth whom He will, is never unjust in what He does, never does anything except of His own free-will, and never wills anything that He does not perform.

Chapter 103. —Interpretation of the Expression in I Tim. II. 4: "Who Will Have All Men to Be Saved."

Accordingly, when we hear and read in Scripture that He "will have all men to be saved," although we know well that all men are not saved, we are not on that account to restrict the omnipotence of God, but are rather to understand the Scripture, "Who will have all men to be saved," as meaning that no man is saved unless God wills his salvation: not that there is no man whose salvation He does not will, but that no man is saved apart from His will; and that, therefore, we should pray Him to will our salvation, because if He will it, it must necessarily be accomplished. And it was of prayer to God that the apostle was speaking when he used this expression. And on the same principle we interpret the expression in the Gospel: "The true light which lightest every man that cometh into the world:" not that there is no man who is not enlightened, but that no man is enlightened except by Him. Or, it is said, "Who will have all men to be saved;" not that there is no man whose salvation He does not will (for how, then, explain the fact that He was unwilling to work miracles in the presence of some who, He said, would have repented if He had worked them?), but that we are to understand by "all men," the human race in all its varieties of rank and circumstances,—kings, subjects; noble, plebeian, high, low, learned, and unlearned; the sound in body, the feeble, the clever, the dull, the foolish, the rich, the poor, and those of middling circumstances; males, females, infants, boys, youths; young, middle-aged, and old men; of every tongue, of every fashion, of all arts, of all professions, with all the innumerable differences of will and conscience, and whatever else there is that makes a distinction among men. For which of all these classes is there out of which God does not will that men should be saved in all nations through His only-begotten Son, our Lord, and therefore does save them; for the Omnipotent cannot will in vain, whatsoever He may will? Now the apostle had enjoined that prayers should be made for all men, and had especially added, "For kings, and for all that are in authority," who might be supposed, in the pride and pomp of worldly station, to shrink from the humility of the Christian faith. Then saying, "For this is good and acceptable in the sight of God our Savior," that is, that prayers should be made for such as these, he immediately adds, as if to remove any ground of despair, "Who will have all men to be saved, and to come unto the knowledge of the truth." God, then, in His great condescension has judged it good to grant to the prayers of the humble the salvation of the exalted; and assuredly we have many examples of this. Our Lord, too, makes use of the same mode of speech in the Gospel, when He says to the Pharisees: "Ye tithe mint, and rue, and every herb." For the Pharisees did not tithe what belonged to others, nor all the herbs of all the inhabitants of other lands. As, then, in this place we must understand by "every herb," every kind of herbs, so in the former passage we may understand by "all men," every sort of men. And we may interpret it in any other way we please, so long as we are not compelled to believe that the omnipotent God has willed anything to be done which was not done: for setting aside all ambiguities, if "He hath done all that He pleased in heaven and in earth," as the psalmist sings of Him, He certainly did not will to do anything that He hath not done.

Chapter 104. —God, Foreknowing the Sin of the First Man, Ordered His Own Purposes Accordingly.

Wherefore, God would have been willing to preserve even the first man in that state of salvation in which he was created, and after he had begotten sons to remove him at a fit time, without the intervention of death, to a better place, where he should have been not only free from sin, but free even from the desire of sinning, if He had foreseen that man would have the steadfast will to persist in the state of innocence in which he was created. But as He foresaw that man would make a bad use of his free-will, that is, would sin, God arranged His own designs rather with a view to do good to man even in his sinfulness, that thus the good will of the Omnipotent might not be made void by the evil will of man, but might be fulfilled in spite of it.

Chapter 105. —Man Was So Created as to Be Able to Choose Either Good or Evil: in the Future Life, the Choice of Evil Will Be Impossible.

Now it was expedient that man should be at first so created, as to have it in his power both to will what was right and to will what was wrong; not without reward if he willed the former, and not without punishment if he willed the latter. But in the future life it shall not be in his power to will evil; and yet this will constitute no restriction on the freedom of his will. On the contrary, his will shall be much freer when it shall be wholly impossible for him to be the slave of sin. We should never think of blaming the will, or saying that it was no will, or that it was not to be called free, when we so desire happiness, that not only do we shrink from misery, but find it utterly impossible to do otherwise. As, then, the soul even now finds it impossible to desire unhappiness, so in future it shall be wholly impossible for it to desire sin. But God's arrangement was not to be broken, according to which He willed to show how good is a rational being who is able even to refrain from sin, and yet how much better is one who cannot sin at all; just as that was an inferior sort of immortality, and yet it was immortality, when it was possible for man to avoid death, although there is reserved for the future a more perfect immortality, when it shall be impossible for man to die.

Chapter 106. —The Grace of God Was Necessary to Man's Salvation Before the Fall as Well as After It.

The former immortality man lost through the exercise of his free-will; the latter he shall obtain through grace, whereas, if he had not sinned, he should have obtained it by desert. Even in that case, however, there could have been no merit without grace; because, although the mere exercise of man's free-will was sufficient to bring in sin, his free-will would not have sufficed for his maintenance in righteousness, unless God had assisted it by imparting a portion of His unchangeable goodness. Just as it is in man's power to die whenever he will (for, not to speak of other means, anyone can put an end to himself by simple abstinence from food), but the mere will cannot preserve life in the absence of food and the other means of life; so man in paradise was able of his mere will, simply by abandoning righteousness, to destroy himself; but to have maintained a life of righteousness would have been too much for his will, unless it had been sustained by the Creator's power. After the fall, however, a more abundant exercise of God's mercy was required, because the will itself had to be freed from the bondage in which it was held by sin and death. And the will owes its freedom in no degree to itself, but solely to the grace of God which comes by faith in Jesus Christ; so that the very will, through which we accept all the other gifts of God which lead us on to His eternal gift, is itself prepared of the Lord, as the Scripture says.

Chapter 107. —Eternal Life, Though the Reward of Good Works, is Itself the Gift of God.

Wherefore, even eternal life itself, which is surely the reward of good works, the apostle calls the gift of God. "For the wages of sin," he says, "is death; but the gift of God is eternal life through Jesus Christ our Lord." Wages (stipendium) is paid as a recompense for military service; it is not a gift: wherefore he says, "the wages of sin is death," to show that death was not inflicted undeservedly, but as the due recompense of sin. But a gift, unless it is wholly unearned, is not a gift at all. We are to understand, then, that man's good deserts are themselves the gift of God, so that when these obtain the recompense of eternal life, it is simply grace given for grace. Man, therefore, was thus made upright that, though unable to remain in his uprightness without divine help, he could of his own mere will depart from it. And whichever of these courses he had chosen, God's will would have been done, either by him, or concerning him. Therefore, as he chose to do his own will rather than God's, the will of God is fulfilled concerning him; for God, out of one and the same heap of perdition which constitutes the race of man, makes one vessel to honor, another to dishonor; to honor in mercy, to dishonor in judgment; that no one may glory in man, and consequently not in himself.

Chapter 108. —A Mediator Was Necessary to Reconcile Us to God; And Unless This Mediator Had Been God, He Could Not Have Been Our Redeemer.

For we could not be redeemed, even through the one Mediator between God and men, the man Christ Jesus, if He were not also God. Now when Adam was created, he, being a righteous man, had no need of a mediator. But when sin had placed a wide gulf between God and the human race, it was expedient that a Mediator, who alone of the human race was born, lived, and died without sin, should reconcile us to God, and procure even for our bodies a resurrection to eternal life, in order that the pride of man might be exposed and cured through the humility of God; that man might be shown how far he had departed from God, when God became incarnate to bring him back; that an example might be set to disobedient man in the life of obedience of the God-Man; that the fountain of grace might be opened by the Only-begotten taking upon Himself the form of a servant, a form which had no antecedent merit; that an earnest of that resurrection of the body which is promised to the redeemed might be given in the resurrection of the Redeemer; that the devil might be subdued by the same nature which it was his boast to have deceived, and yet man not glorified, lest pride should again spring up; and, in fine, with a view to all the advantages which the thoughtful can perceive and describe, or perceive without being able to describe, as flowing from the transcendent mystery of the person of the Mediator.

Chapter 109. —The State of the Soul During the Interval Between Death and the Resurrection.

During the time, moreover, which intervenes between a man's death and the final resurrection, the soul dwells in a hidden retreat, where it enjoys rest or suffers affliction just in proportion to the merit it has earned by the life which it led on earth.

Chapter 110. —The Benefit to the Souls of the Dead from the Sacraments and Alms of Their Living Friends.

Nor can it be denied that the souls of the dead are benefited by the piety of their living friends, who offer the sacrifice of the Mediator, or give alms in the church on their behalf. But these services are of advantage only to those who during their lives have earned such merit, that services of this kind can help them. For there is a manner of life which is neither so good as not to require these services after death, nor so bad that such services are of no avail after death; there is, on the other hand, a kind of life so good as not to require them; and again, one so bad that when life is over they render no help. Therefore, it is in this life that all the merit or demerit is acquired, which can either relieve or aggravate a man's sufferings after this life. No one, then, need hope that after he is dead he shall obtain merit with God which he has neglected to secure here. And accordingly, it is plain that the services which the church celebrates for the dead are in no way opposed to the apostle's words: "For we must all appear before the judgment-seat of Christ; that everyone may receive the things done in his body, according to that he hath done, whether it be good or bad;" for the merit which renders such services as I speak of profitable to a man, is earned while he lives in the body. It is not to everyone that these services are profitable. And why are they not profitable to all, except because of the different kinds of lives that men lead in the body? When, then, sacrifices either of the altar or of alms are offered on behalf of all the baptized dead, they are thank-offerings for the very good, they are propitiatory offerings for the not very bad, and in the case of the very bad, even though they do not assist the dead, they are a species of consolation to the living. And where they are profitable, their benefit consists either in obtaining a full remission of sins, or at least in making the condemnation more tolerable.

Chapter 111. —After the Resurrection There Shall Be Two Distinct Kingdoms, One of Eternal Happiness, the Other of Eternal Misery.

After the resurrection, however, when the final, universal judgment has been completed, there shall be two kingdoms, each with its own distinct boundaries, the one Christ's, the other the devil's; the one consisting of the good, the other of the bad, —both, however, consisting of angels and men. The former shall have no will, the latter no power, to sin, and neither shall have any power to choose death; but the former shall live truly and happily in eternal life, the latter shall drag a miserable existence in eternal death without the power of dying; for the life and the death shall both be without end. But among the former there shall be degrees of happiness, one being more pre-eminently happy than another; and among the latter there shall be degrees of misery, one being more endurably miserable than another.

Chapter 112. —There is No Ground in Scripture for the Opinion of Those Who Deny the Eternity of Future Punishments.

It is in vain, then, that some, indeed very many, make moan over the eternal punishment, and perpetual, unintermitted torments of the lost, and say they do not believe it shall be so; not, indeed, that they directly oppose themselves to Holy Scripture, but, at the suggestion of their own feelings, they soften down everything that seems hard, and give a milder turn to statements which they think are rather designed to terrify than to be received as literally true. For "Hath God" they say, forgotten to be gracious? hath He in anger shut up His tender mercies?" Now, they read this in one of the holy psalms. But without doubt we are to understand it as spoken of those who are elsewhere called "vessels of mercy," because even they are freed from misery not on account of any merit of their own, but solely through the pity of God. Or, if the men we speak of insist that this passage applies to all mankind, there is no reason why they should therefore suppose that there will be an end to the punishment of those of whom it is said, "These shall go away into everlasting punishment;" for this shall end in the same manner and at the same time as the happiness of those of whom it is said, "but the righteous unto life eternal." But let them suppose, if the thought gives them pleasure, that the pains of the damned are, at certain intervals, in some degree assuaged. For even in this case the wrath of God, that is, their condemnation (for it is this, and not any disturbed feeling in the mind of God that is called His wrath), abided upon them; that is, His wrath, though it still remains, does not shut up His tender mercies; though His tender mercies are exhibited, not in putting an end to their eternal punishment, but in mitigating, or in granting them a respite from, their torments; for the psalm does not say, "to put an end to His anger," or, "when His anger is passed by," but "in His anger." Now, if this anger stood alone, or if it existed in the smallest conceivable degree, yet to be lost out of the kingdom of God, to be an exile from the city of God, to be alienated from the life of God, to have no share in that great goodness which God hath laid up for them that fear Him, and hath wrought out for them that trust in Him, would be a punishment so great, that, supposing it to be eternal, no torments that we know of, continued through as many ages as man's imagination can conceive, could be compared with it.

Chapter 113. —The Death of the Wicked Shall Be Eternal in the Same Sense as the Life of the Saints.

This perpetual death of the wicked, then, that is, their alienation from the life of God, shall abide forever, and shall be common to them all, whatever men, prompted by their human affections, may conjecture as to a variety of punishments, or as to a mitigation or intermission of their woes; just as the eternal life of the saints shall abide forever, and shall be common to them all, whatever grades of rank and honor there may be among those who shine with a harmonious effulgence.

Chapter 114. —Having Dealt with Faith, We Now Come to Speak of Hope. Everything that Pertains to Hope is Embraced in the Lord's Prayer.

Out of this confession of faith, which is briefly comprehended in the Creed, and which, carnally understood, is milk for babes, but, spiritually apprehended and studied, is meat for strong men, springs the good hope of believers; and this is accompanied by a holy love. But of these matters, all of which are true objects of faith, those only pertain to hope which are embraced in the Lord's Prayer. For, "Cursed is the man that trusted in man" is the testimony of holy writ; and, consequently, this curse attaches also to the man who trusted in himself. Therefore, except from God the Lord we ought to ask for nothing either that we hope to do well, or hope to obtain as a reward of our good works.

Chapter 115. —The Seven Petitions of the Lord's Prayer, According to Matthew.

Accordingly, in the Gospel according to Matthew the Lord's Prayer seems to embrace seven petitions, three of which ask for eternal blessings, and the remaining four for temporal; these latter, however, being necessary antecedents to the attainment of the eternal. For when we say, "Hallowed be Thy name: Thy kingdom come: Thy will be done in earth, as it is in heaven" (which some have interpreted, not unfairly, in body as well as in spirit), we ask for blessings that are to be enjoyed forever; which are indeed begun in this world, and grow in us as we grow in grace, but in their perfect state, which is to be looked for in another life, shall be a possession for evermore. But when we say, "Give us this day our daily bread: and forgive us our debts, as we forgive our debtors: and lead us not into temptation, but deliver us from evil," who does not see that we ask for blessings that have reference to the wants of this present life? In that eternal life, where we hope to live forever, the hallowing of God's name, and His kingdom, and His will in our spirit and body, shall be brought to perfection, and shall endure to everlasting. But our daily bread is so called because there is here constant need for as much nourishment as the spirit and the flesh demand, whether we understand the expression spiritually, or carnally, or in both senses. It is here too that we need the forgiveness that we ask, for it is here that we commit the sins; here are the temptations which allure or drive us into sin; here, in a word, is the evil from which we desire deliverance: but in that other world there shall be none of these things.

Chapter 116. —Luke Expresses the Substance of These Seven Petitions More Briefly in Five.

But the Evangelist Luke in his version of the Lord's prayer embraces not seven, but five petitions: not, of course, that there is any discrepancy between the two evangelists, but that Luke indicates by his very brevity the mode in which the seven petitions of Matthew are to be understood. For God's name is hallowed in the spirit; and God's kingdom shall come in the resurrection of the body. Luke, therefore, intending to show that the third petition is a sort of repetition of the first two, has chosen to indicate that by omitting the third altogether. Then he adds three others: one for daily bread, another for pardon of sin, another for immunity from temptation. And what Matthew puts as the last petition, "but deliver us from evil," Luke has omitted, to show us that it is embraced in the previous petition about temptation. Matthew, indeed, himself says, "but deliver," not "and deliver," as if to show that the petitions are virtually one: do not this, but this; so that every man is to understand that he is delivered from evil in the very fact of his not being led into temptation.

Chapter 117. —Love, which is Greater Than Faith and Hope, is Shed Abroad in Our Hearts by the Holy Ghost.

And now as to love, which the apostle declares to be greater than the other two graces, that is, than faith and hope, the greater the measure in which it dwells in a man, the better is the man in whom it dwells. For when there is a question as to whether a man is good, one does not ask what he believes, or what he hopes, but what he loves. For the man who loves aright no doubt believes and hopes aright; whereas the man who has not love believes in vain, even though his beliefs are true; and hopes in vain, even though the objects of his hope are a real part of true happiness; unless, indeed, he believes and hopes for this, that he may obtain by prayer the blessing of love. For, although it is not possible to hope without love, it may yet happen that a man does not love that which is necessary to the attainment of his hope; as, for example, if he hopes for eternal life (and who is there that does not desire this?) and yet does not love righteousness, without which no one can attain to eternal life. Now this is the true faith of Christ which the apostle speaks of, "which worketh by love;" and if there is anything that it does not yet embrace in its love, asks that it may receive, seeks that it may find, and knocks that it may be opened unto it. For faith obtains through prayer that which the law commands. For without the gift of God, that is, without the Holy Spirit, through whom love is shed abroad in our hearts, the law can command, but it cannot assist;

and, moreover, it makes a man a transgressor, for he can no longer excuse himself on the plea of ignorance. Now carnal lust reigns where there is not the love of God.

Chapter 118. —The Four Stages of the Christian's Life, and the Four Corresponding Stages of the Church's History.

When, sunk in the darkest depths of ignorance, man lives according to the flesh undisturbed by any struggle of reason or conscience, this is his first state. Afterwards, when through the law has come the knowledge of sin, and the Spirit of God has not yet interposed His aid, man, striving to live according to the law, is thwarted in his efforts and falls into conscious sin, and so, being overcome of sin, becomes its slave ("for of whom a man is overcome, of the same is he brought in bondage"); and thus the effect produced by the knowledge of the commandment is this, that sin worketh in man all manner of concupiscence, and he is involved in the additional guilt of willful transgression, and that is fulfilled which is written: "The, law entered that the offense might abound." This is man's second state. But if God has regard to him, and inspires him with faith in God's help, and the Spirit of God begins to work in him, then the mightier power of love strives against the power of the flesh; and although there is still in the man's own nature a power that fights against him (for his disease is not completely cured), yet he lives the life of the just by faith, and lives in righteousness so far as he does not yield to evil lust, but conquers it by the love of holiness. This is the third state of a man of good hope; and he who by steadfast piety advances in this course, shall attain at last to peace, that peace which, after this life is over, shall be perfected in the repose of the spirit, and finally in the resurrection of the body. Of these four different stages the first is before the law, the second is under the law, the third is under grace, and the fourth is in full and perfect peace. Thus, too, has the history of God's people been ordered according to His pleasure who disposes all things in number, and measure, and weight. For the church existed at first before the law; then under the law, which was given by Moses; then under grace, which was first made manifest in the coming of the Mediator. Not, indeed, that this grace was absent previously, but, in harmony with the arrangements of the time, it was veiled and hidden. For none, even of the just men of old, could find salvation apart from the faith of Christ; nor unless He had been known to them could their ministry have been used to convey prophecies concerning Him to us, some more plain, and some more obscure.

Chapter 119. —The Grace of Regeneration Washes Away All Past Sin and All Original Guilt.

Now in whichever of these four stages (as we may call them) the grace of regeneration finds any particular man, all his past sins are there and then pardoned, and the guilt which he contracted in his birth is removed in his new birth; and so true is it that "the wind bloweth where it listeth," that some have never known the second stage, that of slavery under the law, but have received the divine assistance as soon as they received the commandment.

Chapter 120. —Death Cannot Injure Those Who Have Received the Grace of Regeneration.

But before a man can receive the commandment, it is necessary that he should live according to the flesh. But if once he has received the grace of regeneration, death shall not injure him, even if he should forthwith depart from this life; "for to this end Christ both died, and rose, and revived, that He might be Lord both of the dead and the living;" nor shall death retain dominion over him for whom Christ freely died.

Chapter 121. —Love is the End of All the Commandments, and God Himself is Love.

All the commandments of God, then, are embraced in love, of which the apostle says: "Now the end of the commandment is charity, out of a pure heart, and of a good conscience, and of faith unfeigned." Thus, the end of every commandment is charity, that is, every commandment has love for its aim. But whatever is done either through fear of punishment or from some other carnal motive, and has not for its principle that love which the Spirit of God sheds abroad in the heart, is not done as it ought to be done, however it may appear to men. For this love embraces both the love of God and the love of our neighbor, and "on these two commandments hang all the law and the prophets," we may add the Gospel and the apostles. For it is from these that we hear this voice: The end of the commandment is charity, and God is love. Wherefore, all God's commandments, one of which is, "Thou shalt not commit adultery," and all those precepts which are not commandments but special counsels, one of which is, "It is good for a man not to touch a woman," are rightly carried out only when the motive principle of action is the love of God, and the love of our neighbor in God. And this applies both to the present and the future life. We love God now by faith, then we shall love Him through sight. Now we love even our neighbor by faith; for we who are ourselves mortal know not the hearts of mortal men. But in the future life, the Lord "both will bring to light the hidden things of darkness, and will make manifest the counsels of the hearts, and then shall every man have praise of God;" for every man shall love and praise in his neighbor the virtue which, that it may not be hid, the Lord Himself shall bring to light. Moreover, lust diminishes as love grows, till the latter grows to such a height that it can grow no higher here. For "greater love hath no man than this, that a man lay down his life for his friends." Who then can tell how great love shall be in the future world, when there shall be no lust for it to restrain and conquer? for that will be the perfection of health when there shall be no struggle with death.

Chapter 122. —Conclusion.

But now there must be an end at last to this volume. And it is for yourself to judge whether you should call it a hand-book, or should use it as such. I, however, thinking that your zeal in Christ ought not to be despised, and believing and hoping all good of you in dependence on our Redeemer's help, and loving you very much as one of the members of His body, have, to the best of my ability, written this book for you on Faith, Hope, and Love. May its value be equal to its length.

www.ingramcontent.com/pod-product-compliance
Lightning Source LLC
Chambersburg PA
CBHW052107070526
44584CB00017B/2376